Praise for

Pil

"What a wonderful collection! The ⟨...⟩ ⟨...⟩age is to become a tourist, collecting junk ar⟨...⟩ ⟨...⟩s but is not changed—a pilgrim can stay at hon⟨...⟩ ⟨...⟩aveling towards a goal "whose builder and m⟨...⟩ ⟨...⟩man shares her pilgrimage with us, the insights of a journey that reveal the goal she seeks, which is the true journey of us all, as soon as we leave off being tourists." —Father Stephen Freeman, author of *Everywhere Present: Christianity in a One-Storey Universe*, popular speaker, blogger, and podcaster.

"With crisp prose and vivid descriptions, Susan Cushman's PILGRIM INTERRUPTED delves deeply and unflinchingly into her dogged pursuit of holiness despite being hindered by her own need for healing and redemption. Readers of Madeleine Engle's non-fiction such as *A Circle of Quiet* will love this work." —Jolina Petersheim, bestselling author of *How the Light Gets In*

"Many pilgrims along the way will find in Susan Cushman a very helpful guide for this journey that never ends." —Scott Cairns, author of *Slow Pilgrim: The Collected Poems*, *Short Trip to the Edge: A Pilgrimage to Prayer*, and *Anaphora*

"In this powerful collection, Susan Cushman pulls back the curtain on her most intimate thoughts as she grapples with what it means to be human. From spirituality to trauma, from southern culture to racism, from identity to self-worth, from love to loss. She offers readers an opportunity to see the world through her lens, delivering an authentic, soul-shaping body of work." —Julie Cantrell, New York Times and USA Today bestselling author of *Perennials*

"*Pilgrim Interrupted* reminds me in so many ways of my own messy desire to reach a more holy version of myself, only to discover that it is in my brokenness I find communion with others and begin again on the road to healing. At the core of Susan's being is a longing for the Divine. As such, the lens of her being is always ultimately looking through the eyes of hope, faith, and grace along the ever-changing path of her existence. Without pretense or false promises she invites the reader to join her on the path toward what lies at the end of this world and continues into the next." —River Jordan, *The Ancient Way: Discoveries on the Path of Celtic Christianity*

"A brave book written from the heart and with raw honesty. In *Pilgrim Interrupted* every reader will find parts of themselves as they follow the author's transition through the spiritual, intellectual, and physical stages of life." —Theodore Pitsios, author of *The Bellmaker's House, Searching for Ithaka*, and *Walking in the Light*

"Susan's writing is infused with honesty, humor and grace—as well as with struggle, brokenness and doubt. Her contemplations are bound to the movement and everyday moments of her own life, from the writing of shimmering icons and sublimity of Orthodox chant to reading Flannery O'Connor and listening to Iris Dement. A bold and captivating collection." —Sonja Livingston, author of *The Virgin of Prince Street*

"Having followed Susan Cushman's writing for over a decade, in short stories, novels, essays, and memoir, I am delighted at the way this collection brings together her varied talents and gives us as readers the sense of a life deeply lived, in all its brokenness and beauty. Readers of Brené Brown, Elizabeth Gilbert, and Mary Karr will find solace here, as Cushman encourages us to open ourselves to understanding our own stories, and to live fully into our own becoming." —Jennifer Horne, editor of *All Out of Faith: Southern Women on Spirituality* and *Circling Faith: Southern Women on Spirituality*, author of the poetry collections *Bottle Tree, Little Wanderer,* and *Borrowed Light* and the short story collection *Tell the World You're a Wildflower.* Jennifer was the Poet Laureate of Alabama from 2017-2021.

"The reader becomes the "uninterrupted pilgrim" in Cushman's unflinching yet embracing search. She guilelessly shares a lifetime's pains many would balk at confronting and, ultimately, shows us that brokenness is blessing, the beginning of the pilgrim's path to healing." — Suzanne Smith Henley, author of *Sauce for the Goose* and *Bead by Bead*

"Infused with religious history and spiritual wonder, Susan's personal pilgrimage is informative and engaging. With plain-spoken candor, she reaches and seeks, but doesn't get stuck in the searching. Her peace is made by the art that comes from the questioning. Confession. Consecration. Communion. Creation. Continuance. An act of living art." —Wendy Reed, Emmy award writer and producer for The University of Alabama Center for Public Television and Radio for 20 years, author and editor of numerous books including *An Accidental Memoir—How I Killed Someone and Other Stories*

"Susan Cushman gathers her gifted writing over the years into one exquisitely wrapped package that is now in the shape of a memoir. This collection is a must for writers and all previously privileged to read any of Susan's essays or hear her speak." —The Rev. Joanna J. Seibert M.D., Episcopal deacon, retired physician, and fellow writer

"Memoirists often describe themselves as "spiritual but not religious." Susan Cushman is unapologetically "religious." Her daily life and her creative life are firmly rooted in and set aflame by the rich and sensory spiritual practices of her Orthodox Christian faith. Susan is also a born-and-bred Southern woman. It is the confluence of these two seemingly disparate perspectives that creates a unique collection. Who knew that icons, nail polish, incense, and football games could reside in the psyche of one pilgrim." —Sybil MacBeth is the author of *Praying in Color: Drawing a New Path to God.*

PILGRIM INTERRUPTED

A COLLECTION

SUSAN CUSHMAN

BROTHER MOCKINGBIRD

Other titles by Susan Cushman

John and Mary Margaret
Friends of the Library
Cherry Bomb
Tangles and Plaques: A Mother and Daughter Face Alzheimer's
Southern Writers on Writing
A Second Blooming: Becoming the Women We Are Meant to Be
The Pulpwood Queens Celebrate 20 Years!

Library of Congress Control Number: 2022933573

Cover Design by: Alexios Saskalidis
www.facebook.com/187designz

For information please contact:
Brother Mockingbird, LLC
www.brothermockingbird.org
ISBN: 978-1-7378411-6-6 Paperback
ISBN: 978-1-7378411-7-3 eBook
First Edition

Maybe my brokenness, like the egg yolks that I use to make tempera paint for my icons—themselves a form of life interrupted—is part of my offering to God.

—Susan Cushman, *"Chiaroscuro: Shimmer and Shadow" (Circling Faith: Southern Women on Spirituality, University of Alabama Press, 2012)*

Table of Contents

J'ai Essayé : A Decade of Trying
(Introduction)

I love essays. From 2007-2017 dozens of my essays were published in various anthologies, journals, magazines, newspapers, and blogs, including my own blog, *Pen and Palette*, in which I published three essays a week during that same decade.

The word "essay" comes from the French *essayer*, meaning "to try." Writers *try* to put forth information, opinions, or inspiration—universal or personal—in a nonfiction piece of prose on any subject.

Most of my essays are personal or autobiographical in nature. Many of them are micro-memoir, tiny reflections on personal experiences, based in part on research in religion, art, literature, or mental health.

The French author Michel de Montaigne (1533-1592), possibly the first writer to describe his work as *essays*, said they were "attempts" to put his thoughts into writing. By the 20th century, many professional and aspiring writers, journalists, and academics were using the essay to convey political themes and literary criticism. Accomplished and well-known contemporary American authors such as Joan Didion and Anne Lamott have popularized the essay and set the bar high for those of us who would emulate them.

I didn't set out to write a book of essays. I was looking for a "project" while considering writing a new novel, so I began searching for ideas within the personal essays I had written previously.

As I read through and organized the essays, I began to realize I had written a decade long memoir that seemed to fall into six themes, each reflecting an important part of my life:

Section I, "Icons, Orthodoxy, and Spirituality," contains twelve pieces, including the title essay for the book, "Pilgrim Interrupted," which is set on the Island of Patmos during a pilgrimage to Greece. "Icons Will Save the World," is an early essay that was published in *First Things: The Journal of Religion, Culture, and Public Life*, in 2007. I also included "Blocked" in this section, which was a finalist in the *Santa Fe Writer's Project's* 2008 essay contest, and possibly my personal favorite. And stepping outside the essay genre, I've included a poem here, as well as in a couple of other sections.

The seven pieces in Section II, "Writing, Editing, and Publishing," offer a peek into my personal writing world.

Section III, "Alzheimer's, Caregiving, Death, and Dying," includes "Hitting the Wall," for which I received excellent feedback from *The Paris Review* in 2010, but for some reason I set it aside and did not work on it again until I decided to include it in this collection. I added two excerpts from my novel *John and Mary Margaret* to this section, although they aren't essays. "Walker, Alzheimer's, and Sunset Park" and "Elizabeth and Lewy Body Dementia" are fictional, but are inspired by the loss of my mother, with Alzheimer's, in 2016, and my dear friend Nancy, with Lewy Body Dementia in 2020.

Section IV—"Family and Adoption"—is a small grouping of personal family stories. Most of these are nonfiction, but I chose to include the short story, "Avery," here. This story from my collection, *Friends of the Library*, is inspired by my two adopted sons, Jonathan and Jason.

Section V—"Place"—contains reflections on setting in southern literature, experiences in small towns in Mississippi, scenes in a monastery and at an opera, and two poems.

The collection closes out with Section VI—"Mental Health, Addiction, and Sexual Abuse"—which contains candid explorations of my struggles with eating disorders, depression, and recovery from sexual abuse.

While I hope that few of my readers have these difficulties, I do hope that many have experienced the thrill of creating a piece of art, or writing an exciting sentence or paragraph or essay or book, or the ecstasy that a genuine religious experience can produce. As my friend, the author Lee Smith says, "I do feel, when I'm writing at a fever pitch, that intensity that you feel when you get saved. There's nothing else that makes you feel like that. There's getting saved, sex, and writing."

The poems I've included in *Pilgrim Interrupted* aren't essays, of course, but they do reflect effort. In writing them, *I tried* (J'ai essayé) to capture the emotional impact of various life experiences. The artwork illustrating the poem "Wide Margins" is also my own. I spent a few months with a group of artists who gathered monthly to work on art and drink wine and encourage each other. I did the gouache illustration for this poem at one of those meetings of the "Mixed Bag Ladies" back in August of 2007.

The icons in this book were all written by me, using the ancient method of painting with egg tempera on wood panels covered with gesso. Several of the essays explain more about this liturgical art form and my experiences studying it, doing commissioned pieces, teaching workshops, and eventually leaving it behind to pursue a full-time writing career. Those experiences were an important part of the inspiration for my novel *Cherry Bomb*, (published in 2017) in which a weeping icon of Saint Mary of Egypt plays a major role. The protagonist, Mare, studies iconography at a workshop at an Orthodox monastery, as I had done numerous times. And she sees weeping icons firsthand, as I also did on several occasions. (She also throws up graffiti on buildings in a small town in Georgia, something I haven't actually experienced personally, although I donned a hoody and lined our backyard fence with butcher paper and threw up "Mare's" tag, to try to get into the graffiti spirit.)

Essays, excerpts from my novels and blog, poetry, and numerous icons and other pieces of original art are all included here. I hope there's something here for everyone to reflect on, and that my readers will find some measure of joy or inspiration from the journey I've shared. My pilgrimage—mostly in the "Christ-haunted South"—has definitely been interrupted over the decades of my life, but hopefully the prose, poetry, and art that litter the pathway are of some value.

I

ICONS, ORTHODOXY AND SPIRITUALITY

Standing before the icon of Christ in the front of St. John Orthodox Church, I prepare to offer my confession at the Sacrament of Forgiveness. The Holy image of the One Who Forgives comes forth to meet me, as the father comes forth to welcome home the prodigal son in the familiar gospel passage (Luke 15:11-32). The love of Jesus pours forth from His prototype (the icon), sees the offering of my broken heart, and raises it to the Heavenly realm.

—Susan Cushman, *from "Icons Will Save the World," published in First Things: The Journal of Religion, Culture, and Public Life, December 20, 2007*

Sometimes I stop and look at the unfinished images with a melancholy longing. The other day I paused before the icon of Christ, fingering a soft sable brush and scanning the jars of pigments on the nearby shelves. There are eggs in the refrigerator, waiting to be broken for Him. Their yolks, themselves a type of life interrupted, are ready to bind the dry pigments and fill my palette with a range of ochres and siennas for the face of Christ. Everything I need is here, waiting for my touch.

—Susan Cushman, *from "Blocked" (published in the Santa Fe Writers Project, literary awards finalist, July 2, 2008)*

Chiaroscuro: Shimmer and Shadow
2012

How a spiritual expat from the "Christ-haunted South" found healing through art and Eastern Orthodoxy

Growing up in Jackson, Mississippi, in the 1950s and '60s, I was always attracted to powerful religious experiences. From my childhood years in the Presbyterian Church, through my involvement with religious movements on college campuses, and finally the Jesus freak hippies that formed a church in my first apartment, I finally landed within the walls of the ancient Orthodox Christian Church in the 1980s. It is no small thing to leave one's religious upbringing, especially in the South, for something as foreign as Eastern Orthodoxy. With this conversion came lots of changes, and the process continues today.

Head Coverings and Nuns

First I changed my name. I chose Mary of Egypt as my patron saint early in my conversion, changing my name from Susan to "Marye," and adding the "e" for Egypt, a way of distinguishing her from Mary the Mother of God and other saints who share her name. I began signing all my correspondence, "forgive me, Marye, the sinner," and naively used "sinfulmarye" as part of my original e-mail address. You can imagine the spam that hit my in-box.

My husband had become a priest in the Antiochian Orthodox

Church, and so, to add to the peculiarity of my new nomenclature, I started using the Church's traditional title for a priest's wife—khouriya—introducing myself in church circles and taking communion as Khouriya Marye.

Then I started covering my head in church. While head coverings are common in countries where Orthodoxy is indigenous, they're rare in America, especially in the South, even in our Orthodox churches. But the custom was cropping up in some convert parishes, and soon a half-dozen or so women at Memphis's Saint John Orthodox Church were covering their heads during worship. I'm sure my close friends and family were wondering where it would all lead.

And then I met the nuns.

Everything about Holy Dormition Monastery reflected a high level of care and attention to detail. The grounds were meticulously maintained, mostly by the nuns themselves, with some help from visitors. On one of my visits I asked if I could help clean the chapel. The nun assigned to the task showed me how to clean the iconostasis, the icons themselves, and some of the altarware used during services. We cleaned the windows, dusted the chairs, and lifted the oriental rugs to clean underneath them before lying them flat and vacuuming them, with special attention to straightening out the fringe on the ends.

"So, how often do you do such a thorough cleaning in here?" I asked, thinking this must have been a spring cleaning of sorts.

She looked at me as though she hadn't quite heard me. "Every Saturday."

The nuns didn't wait for the house of the Lord to get dirty before cleaning it. They kept it clean always, the way we should care for our souls.

The same nuns who had been busy cleaning and gardening and cooking and sewing vestments and painting icons and welcoming

visitors during the day quickly found their way into the chapel at the
sound of the wooden hammer rhythmically beating on the seman-
tron—the gong-like instrument that called us to prayer—and the ringing of the bells before the evening service. When I entered the darkened
nave, my eyes adjusted slowly to the candlelight, and my other senses
came alive. All around was the sweet pungency of incense. As I took in
the shimmering gold leaf of the icons, I realized the nuns were singing
beautiful Romanian melodies whose words I couldn't understand but
whose sense I somehow felt. After asking a blessing from the abbess, the
nuns took turns at the reader's stand. The ones who weren't chanting
often prostrated themselves, rolling gracefully into little black balls on
their knees for long periods of time, their faces to the floor.

The first time I heard them sing, I felt like Prince Vladimir's
envoys to Hagia Sophia in Constantinople near the end of the tenth
century must have felt. They had been sent to find a religion that Vladimir could embrace and offer to the people of Russia. After visiting the
great cathedral, they reported, "We didn't know whether we were in
Heaven or on earth." Although I had been Orthodox for six years before my first visit to a monastery, my experience of Orthodox worship
up until then had been limited, for the most part, to my convert parish,
which was still learning the ways of this ancient religion. The nuns
at the monastery had grown up with the Orthodox faith—it flowed
through them organically. They sounded like angels. Especially Mother
Gabriella, whom I often refer to as simply "Mother."

I fell in love with Mother the first time I met her. This beautiful
Romanian nun was about my age, and we had both married when we
were only nineteen. But she married *Jesus*. Thirty years later she found
herself serving as abbess of an active monastery that kept the traditional schedule of more than six hours of church services daily, while
welcoming Orthodox clergy and hierarchs on a regular basis, serving

dinner for up to a hundred guests most Sundays, maintaining a cemetery, a vegetable garden, a vestment-sewing business, an icon studio,
and caring for visitors in its guest house year-round. In the midst of
this busy schedule, Mother always took time to meet with her spiritual
children from the outside world. She took me on; and, as I became a
student of iconography in the monastery's classes taught by Russian
iconographers, Mother Gabriella's guidance never wavered.

Painting Icons: Writing the Lives of the Saints in Color

Iconography is spiritual work. It involves adherence to ancient canons
regarding style, content, and even the choice of colors for the various
subjects illustrated. After my first three workshops, I became frustrated
with the harshness of the Russian instructors, so with Mother's blessing
I traveled to numerous other places to study under iconographers from
Greece and the United States. Eventually, I found my way back to the
monastery to take a class under one of the Romanian nuns. For the next
few years I explored a variety of these styles, always using egg tempera
and gold leaf.

I painted dozens of icons over the next several years, and even
began doing commissioned pieces, giving lectures on iconography,
leading workshops at my church, and teaching classes in my studio at
home. Iconography opened the door for me to find my way back to
art—especially to writing. Or maybe I should say it was a way for me to
come in the *back door* to art. As a spiritual discipline, it was looked upon
favorably by the church and, more importantly, by my pastor and my
husband, both of whom I still desperately wanted to please. It would be
a few more years before I would take the next step towards self-realiza-
tion as an artist. But first, I had more work to do on my wounded psyche.

Wisdom From a Spiritual Mother

It was the last day of my pilgrimage, and Mother had asked me to wait for her after lunch, on a bench under a tree that overlooked the vegetable garden. I always anticipated these talks with a mixture of anxiety and hope, as one might feel before a surgical procedure that held potential for great healing.

I sat on the bench, admiring the beauty of the sloping grounds, surrounded by deep woods which formed a protective border around the back of the monastery property. This was Michigan, and the pleasant breeze held none of the stifling heat of summers in the South. The Mother of God flower garden was in full bloom and the vegetable garden was at its peak. As I waited for Mother to join me, I thought about what I would say to her this time . . . which struggles I would place in the light of her compassionate wisdom. She knew me well, having been my guide through various stages of my (ongoing) recovery from sexual abuse, eating disorders, and various addictive behaviors. She was always a safe place for me to land with my anger, especially when it was directed at the Church and its hierarchy. Yes, this spiritual home that I had found after my seventeen-year journey wasn't perfect. It was filled with broken people, just like me. But my experiences growing up with abuse and not finding safety even within the walls of the Church had left me in a messy and continuing battle with forgiveness.

Just as I was forming these thoughts for my talk with Mother, I noticed one of the nuns pulling weeds in the garden. This struck me as odd, because I knew they were excused from physical labor on Sundays, other than the necessary tasks of preparing meals and cleaning rooms in the guest house for incoming visitors. Bent over in her long black habit which covered every inch of her skin other than her face and hands, the nun labored meticulously, her works—and her very identity—hidden from the world's view. It was only when she turned and began walking up the hill towards the bench where I was sitting that I recognized her. Yes, the abbess of the monastery was pulling weeds in the vegetable garden. She approached me with a smile and sat beside me under the shade tree, placing the weeds on the ground at her feet to take care of later. I think she would have sat there silently for a long while if I hadn't hurried the conversation.

"So, how's your arthritis?"

"Thank God. It's not too bad today. Some of the sisters have had more pain with the cleanup work after last month's storm."

The day before I had seen an elderly nun driving a tractor, hauling broken tree limbs and other debris to the back of the property. I felt so bad for her that I offered to help, but after an hour or two, I was worn out and returned to the guest house to rest up for the evening's four-hour church service. But the old nun kept working right up until the bell range for Vigil, when she climbed down from the tractor and headed into the chapel and approached the reader's stand for her shift as chanter.

"What's that?" Mother asked, pointing to the book in my lap that I had discovered in the monastery bookstore earlier in the week.

"It's Father Webber's new book, *The Steps of Transformation*. You know it?"

She nodded. "I think it does a good job of putting the Twelve Steps into an Orthodox framework. You finished or just starting?"

"Started it just since I've been here. It's . . . helpful. But, you know, as far as I've come in healing my lifelong wounds—through the sacraments and prayer and self-help books—it seems like I've still got an itch I can't quite scratch. I was wondering . . . do you think therapy would help?"

Mother was silent for a minute before speaking. She often did this, pausing to finger the knots in her prayer rope.

"It might, but the thing you have to be careful about with modern-day psychology is the temptation to think you can fix everything in this life. Some things might not get completely healed this side of Heaven. Maybe that itch is there to remind you that God's grace is perfect in our weakness. It's fine to seek healing, but we also have to learn to live with brokenness."

The Middle Way: Finding Balance

Mother had watched my spiritual metamorphosis from "Khouriya Marye" with my monastic yearnings for several years, back to "Susan," as I reclaimed my given name and focused my energies on finding balance.

After about five years of what some of my friends called my "nun phase," I took off my head covering and embraced my southern roots. Manicures, makeup, and jewelry returned to my arsenal, and my long-neglected hair again received layered haircuts and blond highlights. The "new me" wasn't as glamorous as some of my Arab-American girlfriends, but I was making a move towards the center, and it began to feel good.

Soon after that visit I was asked to speak at a women's retreat hosted by an Orthodox parish in Austin, Texas. I chose as my topic "The Middle Way: Finding Balance in Our Lives."

One of the talks I gave at the retreat was titled "Women Saints Who Found the Middle Way." Instead of recounting stories from the lives of saints who had lived in extreme poverty or who had experienced brutal martyrdoms while trying to preserve their virginity, I talked about married saints who served God in the everyday business of getting meals for their families, caring for the sick, and burying the dead. Rather than sharing the amazing but bizarre life of my own patron, Saint Mary of Egypt, I chose to speak of Saint Julianna the Merciful and Salome the Myrrhbearer, encouraging my listeners to find joy in living more conventional lives.

As John Maximovitch, the contemporary Russian Orthodox saint, said: "For all the 'mysticism' of our Orthodox Church that is found in the lives of the Saints and the writings of the Holy Fathers, the truly Orthodox person always has both feet on the ground, facing whatever situation is right in front of him. It is in accepting given situations, which requires a loving heart, that one encounters God."

So there I stood with this group of Orthodox women beside a river on a beautiful ranch just outside Austin, trying to keep my feet firmly planted. As I returned to Memphis, refreshed by my encounters with my new friends in Texas, I found another group of women waiting to guide the next steps of my journey.

STRONG WOMEN OF PASSION

In October of 2006 I attended the Southern Festival of Books at the Cook Convention Center, just a few minutes from my home in midtown Memphis. The program boasted a few of my favorite authors, especially Cassandra King, whose book, *The Sunday Wife*, had begun to soften the hard layers with which I had adorned my public persona. Meeting King, sharing my story with her, and having her write in my copy of her book, "To Susan, who knows what a Sunday wife is," were defining moments for me. I loved her even more after I read her essay, "The Making of a Preacher's Wife," in the first volume of *All Out of Faith: Southern Women on Spirituality*. She described her struggle—"balancing a

Southern Belle, good-little-girl persona with that of an artsy wannabe who smoked cigarettes and dreamed of being a writer." And she wrote candidly about her years as a minister's wife, during which she "wrote devotionals and religious poems and church pageants, not out of devotion and true piety, but to please and impress others." Finally she "went underground" and wrote a novel about a preacher's wife who questions her life on many levels, stating that "the writing of it was my salvation."

As I listened to King and the other women on the panel for *All Out of Faith*, my heart was beating so loudly in my chest that I was afraid everyone in the room could hear it. On the inside flap of the book's cover, I read these words: "The South is often considered patriarchal, but as these writers show, Southern culture has always reserved a special place for strong women of passion." *That's me*, I thought. And in the Afterword, the book's editors Jennifer Horne and Wendy Reed wrote about how "spirituality is not removed from ordinary life but infuses it," and about the need to "go inside myself, below the roles I'd taken on as layers." *Yes.*

During the festival I also met Lee Smith, who was reading from her latest work, *On Agate Hill*, and the poet Beth Ann Fennelly, who paints a vivid picture of her own take on womanhood and spirituality in her poetry. She was reading from her latest book of poems, *Tender Hooks*. My favorite poem in that book is "Waiting For the Heart to Moderate," in which she describes what it feels like to be "all edges, on tender hooks" at every stage of a woman's life and to still feel the music "booming in her breastbone." I'm much older than Beth Ann, but I still hear that music, and like her, in my own efforts "to free it," I also worry that I "might do something stupid." But maybe my middle-aged heart is finally learning to moderate.

As the festival ended, I found myself thinking, where have these women been all my life? I hurried home with my autographed treasures and pored myself into the strong but tender female wisdom between the pages of their works. I rediscovered Sue Monk Kidd's writing, especially *The Dance of the Dissident Daughter*. And while my Orthodox embrace of the Mother of God differs from Kidd's approach to the "feminine imagery of the Divine," I benefitted greatly from her wisdom concerning Favored Daughters who "carry the wound of feminine inferiority," trying to make up for it by setting "perfectionist standards . . . A thin body, happy children, an impressive speech, and a perfectly written article."

WRITING MY WAY TO WHOLENESS

Or maybe a perfectly crafted *book*. Three short months after my encounter with these strong women of faith, I completed a novel. But it was a thinly veiled attempt at hiding my truth in the lives of the fictional characters I invented. And since I had an agenda, the characters weren't free to chase the creative rabbit trails they longed to pursue. So I laid them gently on a shelf (to be resurrected later) and I began to write my stories and submit them to literary journals and magazines. In just over a year I had seven personal essays published, so I strapped on my courage and began the work that had begged for an audience from the beginning—a memoir. A year later I realized I wasn't ready to go public with all aspects of my history, so I abandoned the memoir and returned to fiction. My current novel-in-progress features three strong women of passion as its protagonists. I don't know if the writing of it will be my salvation, but it is, at a minimum, an effort towards wholeness.

As the late Madeleine L'Engle said: "Until we have been healed, we do not know what wholeness is: the discipline of creation, be it to paint, compose, or write, is an effort towards wholeness. . . . The important thing is to remember that our gift, no matter what the size, is indeed something given us and which we must humbly serve, and in serving, learn more wholeness, be offered wondrous newness."

Learning to serve the gift through writing and painting is bringing wondrous newness into my life every day. Once it surfaced in an essay about how anger blocked me from painting icons, and how the beach, a dream, and a soft rock song helped me get unblocked. At other times that newness has shown up to cheer me on as I embrace the darker aspects of my Mississippi childhood by laying down difficult chapters of my novel-in-progress. Sometimes I feel its presence during the sacrament of confession, when I've been up all night facing down my demons as I write, often chasing them with vodka or wine. Maybe my brokenness, like the egg yolks that I use to make tempera paint for my icons—themselves a form of life interrupted—is part of my offering to God.

BLOCKED
2008

They've been waiting for months now, like patients on an organ do-nor list. Two large icons—one of Christ, the Life Giver, and another, The Mother of God, Directress—sit unfinished in my studio. A few well-meaning students have offered encouragements like, "Oh, they're almost finished," and "I love the blue highlights on Christ's inner gar-ment." But the images are suspended… like embryos stuck in the birth canal. Their faces are expressionless masks; their lips, a ghoulish, green sankir, thirsty for a wash of vermillion red. Their eyes, empty and pale, waiting for the life-giving lights and distinctive black lines which are the trademarks of this ancient Byzantine art form.

My studio is upstairs, making it easier to avoid the anxious stares of my orphaned pieces. About once a week when I'm forced to walk through the second story landing to attend to some business in one of the upstairs bedrooms, I hear them calling out, like neglected children: "Why have you left us? Is there something wrong with us?"

Sometimes I stop and look at the unfinished images with a mel-ancholy longing. The other day I paused before the icon of Christ, fingering a soft sable brush and scanning the jars of pigments on the nearby shelves. There are eggs in the refrigerator, waiting to be broken for Him. Their yolks, themselves a type of life interrupted, are ready to bind the dry pigments and fill my palette with a range of ochres and siennas for the face of Christ. Everything I need is here, waiting for my touch.

Icons in various stages of completion, models used for instruction, surround me. A finished icon of the Archangel Gabriel watches over the desks and work tables arranged along the banisters overlooking the den below. The cathedral ceiling slants down towards the studio and provides natural light through two well-placed sky lights. Closing my eyes, I can see a procession of icons that have come to life on this desk over the years—saints, angels, martyrs, and various types of the Mother of God and Her Son. Opening my eyes to the work on the table that beckons me, I fight back tears, take a deep breath, and walk away. I feel like the Rich Young Ruler when he discovered, with great sorrow, that he wasn't up to the task. He wasn't able to sell everything to follow Christ.

Much has been written about writer's block. We are told to "just do it"—to write *something* every day. Blocked on that next chapter of your novel? Stuck on a shifting point of view in a short story? Struggling with ethical issues in an essay? No problem. Set it aside and write a journal entry instead. Or just write whatever comes to mind. You can always revise it later.

Unfortunately, writing icons isn't like that. *(Painting icons is called "writing" because you are writing the life of the saint with pigment.)* It's not about *what* to write. It's about *how*… about being *prepared*. Really, it's like approaching the sacrament of Holy Communion. It's spiritual work, bringing these sacred images to life. All icons are sacred, but these two on the tables in my studio are intended for the nave of a church. People will venerate them. They will bow before them and kiss them and light candles to put beside them. Smoke, like incense, will rise to heaven with their prayers.

So what's blocking me? It would be easy to make excuses. I've been busy with other things—writing, caring for a dying friend, traveling. But the truth is, we usually make time for the things that matter most, don't we? Writing is fun. Caring for the sick is rewarding. Traveling is exciting, and can also be a great escape from real life.

My husband and I just got home from a twelve-day trip to Greece. It was part vacation, part spiritual pilgrimage. We visited many Orthodox churches and monasteries, prayed before the tombs of numerous saints, and venerated scores of icons—some ancient, some miracle-working, and some, simply beautiful. My favorites were actually contemporary works done by the nuns at the Monastery Evangelismos on the island of Patmos. The master iconographer, Mother Olympia, studied under Fotios Kontoglou (d.1965), my favorite contemporary Greek iconographer.

Mother Olympia's work is prevalent in churches all over Europe. Before she died, she taught several nuns at the monastery, and their work fills the Catholicon (main church) now. As Sister Tabitha gave us a tour, she pointed out the large wall painting of the Dormition of the Mother of God, saying that most of it was painted by the nuns, the students, but that the *face* of the Holy Virgin was done by Mother Olympia. Writings about her speak of her deep spiritual life, which shows in her icons. They have an other-worldly beauty, a mystical quality that comes from her closeness to God. She was prepared.

Early in the history of the Church, most all iconographers were monastics. They lived secluded lives—away from the cares and temptations of the world—probably more disciplined than mine. You really shouldn't paint icons if you're not at peace in your soul.

Perhaps my own sinfulness is blocking my way upstairs to finish these two icons. Students are calling and emailing to ask the dates of my next workshop. I don't have an answer for them. I've been stirred up for several months, allowing some hurtful interactions and difficult situations to disturb my peace. The high road in Orthodox spirituality involves quietly receiving insults, rejection, and even abuse with thankfulness. Humility is the goal, not the praise of men. This self-effacing approach to life goes against the grain of modern secular psychology. It's an acquired taste, learned through self-denial and the thankful acceptance of suffering.

The life-coach writing for *Real Simple* magazine would probably tell me to walk away from the difficult relationships that are causing my pain. She might tell me to use my anger to fuel my work… to paint or to write through my pain. Some of the Psalms of the Prophet King David, who suffered much pain at the hands of others and as a consequence for his own sins, are full of anguish. Of remorse. But… *anger*?

So, I turned to poetry. First I wrote "Benched," which pretty much described how I was feeling at the time.

Next I explored the possibility of needing to broaden my circle of friends and find kindred spirits in new realms, so I wrote a poem called "Wide Margins." It was about outsider artists and people who are marginalized by society, which was how I was feeling. This one cried out for a louder venue, so I hand-printed the poem on hot press watercolor paper and illustrated it with gouache, with encouragement from a group of fellow artists at our monthly gathering.

Finally, I wrote one that explores the healing of the pain and anger in verse. I called it "Growing Pains."

When the poetry doesn't work, I drink… usually just enough to take the edge off. Alcohol offers a few hours of numbness, but sadly, the receptors for pain are also conduits for creativity.

Sobriety—it's about more than not being drunk. It's clear-eyed brush strokes and poetry that knocks your socks off and page-turning prose. It's Iris Dement singing, "I choose to take my sorrow straight," and Natalie Maines (of the Dixie Chicks) turning a personal affront into a hit song with, "I'm Not Ready to Make Nice." It's Mary Chapin Carpenter singing, "forgiveness doesn't come with a debt." But it's also allowing yourself to be human, and turning that broken humanity into something redemptive with every stroke of your pen or brush or keyboard.

"I'm mad as hell!" Maines croons. So, was she mad when she wrote the lyrics? Was she still mad when she recorded the song? Virginia Woolf said one shouldn't write while angry—that it destroys all chance of objectivity, or something like that. It was in her book, *A Room of One's Own*. She was talking about how Charlotte Bronte's anger hurt the integrity of her work in *Jane Eyre*. (Must not have hurt it too badly… I think there are still a few copies of the book in circulation today.) But Woolf's point, as I remember, was that anger blocks the writer's view of her characters… of her story. That she will end up writing about *herself* instead of them.

If that's true of fiction, how much more important is that concept when it comes to the spiritual work of iconography? If I can't take communion when I'm angry (and I've abstained quite a few times recently,) how can I paint the face of the Mother of God, or of Her Son? Can I just offer myself, warts and all, and climb the stairs to my studio "just as I am"? Would God accept the sacrifice of my art even if it's offered with unclean hands? For that matter, when would my hands ever be clean enough?

It's a Catch 22, much like the great hunger and thirst I feel for the Body and Blood of Jesus on the Sunday mornings when I'm not prepared to receive it, either because I didn't keep the liturgical fast or because I didn't let go of anger and seek reconciliation first. Seems like that's when we need God's healing the most, when we're suffering the consequences of our own sin. But the Mystical Supper isn't a sloppy affair. It's not a "come as you are" event. It's a feast, and wedding garments are requested. If we lower the Holy Eucharist to the standards of a fast food drive through, it will no longer be Holy. So, how do I get unblocked?

There was a prostitute in fifth century Egypt named Mary. She loved all the wrong stuff. She even got on a ship full of pilgrims bound for Jerusalem to venerate the true Cross, which had been placed in a church there. Her purpose on the voyage was to find customers, and she did, indeed, defile many a young boy on that tumultuous ocean voyage. But upon arrival in Jerusalem, she began to be curious about their faith, and tried to follow the crowds into the church. As she attempted to step over the threshold, an invisible force blocked her way. It wasn't just because she was a prostitute—God knows how many of us have sold out to people or things or ideas in this life. It was because she was unrepentant.

After several failed attempts, she fell on her knees before an icon of the Mother of God outside the door to the church, asking forgiveness and begging entry. Her repentance was accepted, and after entering the church to venerate the Cross, Mary spent the rest of her life as a hermit in the desert, away from the things and people she had used and abused. It was her path to salvation… to healing.

Like Saint Mary of Egypt, I often cling to the things that feed my appetite for pleasure… including anger, because anger feels better than pain. And for some time now, like Natalie Maines, I've not been "ready to make nice." But oh, how I long to finish those icons. To climb the steps to my studio and fall on my knees and ask God to take away whatever is blocking me. Maybe I'll do this soon.

But just as I was almost ready to make nice, I suffered another hit. Unintentional, but even accidental gashes hurt, especially when the scab is still new. So, I took off for the beach, where I could stand beside the ocean and be reminded of my smallness. Two days… alone. On the drive down to Gulf Shores I talked with a friend on my cell phone and told her about the dream I had the night before:

Walking on the side of a mountain with a group of travelers,

I leave a gate open and a small child falls off the cliff. Certain that I've caused her death, nausea overtakes me, and grief. The child's parents find her, miraculously alive, later on in the dream. I approach them to share their joy, but they shun me. Their cold, unforgiving looks freeze my heart.

In the same dream, my Goddaughter, Hannah, who is (also in real life) pregnant, delivers twin boys. So my friend (on the cell phone) tells me this:

In dreams, death is often a good thing. The child that fell off the side of the mountain could be my ego. The source of my anger. My pain. It almost died, which is good. But we are never completely free of ego (pride) in this life. But the dream shows that I'm moving towards letting go of the anger. I'm closer to being ready to make nice. Thanks, in part, to the *twins*.

Yes, the twin boys represent my masculine side—my strength—which is fueling my two passions, writing prose and icons. When I let the anger (ego) die, I'll be able to approach the icons again.

But why Hannah? In my dream, Hannah represents purity of heart, and also God's mercy. Hannah has known suffering in her young life, and has overcome many difficult obstacles without becoming bitter. It is not insignificant that she is the bearer of the male twin boys in my dream. Hannah was actually visited by the Mother of God when she was a child. Humility attracts the grace of God.

As I write these words, waves are lapping the beach a few feet away. It's my last day here, and I feel the push and pull of the ocean, of life forces so much larger than my anger. I let them pull the anger away, and I remember the words of a song I heard last night at a restaurant in Gulf Shores. The song was "Let Go," and the songwriter, Bud Smith, sang it with an upbeat attitude, tempered with the humility of lessons learned. I find myself singing it now—*when you're walking through your day, let go.*

It almost sounds trite to say that a soft rock song and the beach could play such a big part in something as important as letting go of anger. But they did. I'm home now, and as I walked up stairs today I found the way to my icons was open. The anger is mostly gone, and I'll start to paint again soon. I'll probably go to Confession first (it's therapeutic, not juridical) and get started next week, but I've begun the process, the preparation.

One of my favorite writers, the late Madeleine L'Engle, said:

Until we have been healed, we do not know what wholeness is: the discipline of creation, be it to paint, compose, or write, is an effort towards wholeness….
The important thing is to remember that our gift, no matter what the size, is indeed something given us and which we must humbly serve, and in serving, learn more wholeness, be offered wondrous newness.

An effort towards wholeness. I can do that. What a relief to learn that I don't have to be healed in order to seek wholeness. Hopefully, I'll be seeking it the rest of my life. And acquiring a taste for humility. But at least for today, I'm ready to make nice. And paint icons.

Icons Will Save the World
2007

Standing before the icon of Christ in the front of St. John Orthodox Church, I prepare to offer my confession at the Sacrament of Forgiveness. The Holy image of the One Who Forgives comes forth to meet me, as the father comes forth to welcome home the prodigal son in the familiar gospel passage (Luke 15:11-32). The love of Jesus pours forth from His prototype (the icon), sees the offering of my broken heart, and raises it to the Heavenly realm.

After receiving the priest's counsel and absolution, I remain in the nave (the large part of the temple, called the "sanctuary" in Protestant churches) to give thanks and to let God's grace and peace fill my heart. Surrounded by icons of Christ, His Mother, the angels, saints, Biblical scenes and Church feasts, I think about how Prince Vladimir's envoys must have felt when they walked into Hagia Sophia Orthodox Cathedral in Constantinople near the end of the tenth century. Their mission was to find a religion that Prince Vladimir could embrace and offer to the people of Russia. In their report they said, "We didn't know whether we were in Heaven or on earth." Shortly thereafter, Orthodoxy became the official religion of Kievan Russia, infusing the lives of peasants and princes, artists and writers with the Orthodox vision of beauty. Nine hundred years later, the Russian writer, Fyodor Dostoevsky, penned the famous words, "Beauty will save the world."

I don't think Prince Vladimir or Dostoevsky had in mind the kind of worldly beauty that today's fashion and entertainment industries worship, or even the beauty of secular art and architecture. I think they were both swept off their feet by true *spiritual* beauty—in Vladimir's case, the beauty of the Orthodox temple (church), adorned with *icons*.

Spiritual Beauty

In his book, *Icons: Theology in Color*, N. Trubetskoi said that the beauty of the icon is *spiritual*. "Our icon painters," Trubetskoi said, "had seen the beauty that would save the world and immortalized it in colors." While he was clearly writing about icons, Dostoevsky didn't limit his definition of beauty to icons. I think he was speaking of incarnational beauty that is found in the works of God's hands *and* in the beauty of his creatures' works.

We are innately creative, because we are made in the image of a creative God. As the twentieth century abstract painter Vassily Kandinsky said, we all strive to make "beauty and order from the chaos of the fallen world." Our Creator has given us the freedom to do this, but sadly, many artists and writers abuse this freedom. The results of that abuse are often pornographic, or at best, self-serving *exposés* masquerading as art or literature.

Good secular art, music, literature, and architecture serve to refine and form our souls and make them better disposed to *spiritual* or *liturgical* art, music, literature, and architecture. In an essay by Father Seraphim Rose called "Forming Young Souls," (*Father Seraphim Rose: His Life and Works*, 2003) he encouraged parents to expose their children to what he calls the "Dushevni Diet"—that which feeds the *middle part of the soul*. "The education of youth today, especially in America, is notoriously deficient in developing responsiveness to the best expressions of human art, literature, and music." His premise is that people raised on such a "diet" would be better prepared to receive the higher, or spiritual foods. Perhaps they would have developed an appetite for the patient work of prayer, worship, and yes, venerating icons.

VENERATION VS WORSHIP

When I converted to Orthodoxy from a Protestant faith (a seventeen year process culminating in 1987), I embraced the *veneration* of icons, unreservedly. An important distinction needs to be made here between *veneration* and *worship*—one better made by St. John of Damascus (A.D. 730, *On the Divine Images*). St John used the term *latreia* for the *absolute* worship reserved only for God, and the word *proskinesis* to describe the *relative* worship, or *veneration*, given to the Mother of God, saints, and sacred objects such as relics and icons. Maybe an analogy from everyday life will help make these definitions easier to grasp.

My father died in 1998. For forty-nine years my parents shared a strong Christian faith—an *adoration* of God—and a strong love and respect for one another. During the last few years of their marriage they developed a morning ritual. Upon waking, they would greet each other with the Psalmist's words, "This is the day the Lord has made," and the response, "Let us rejoice and be glad in it." After my father's death, my mother continued the tradition, greeting instead his *photograph*—an *image* of her husband—often with a kiss, and would say both the greeting and response they once shared. The love and veneration she shows to the image is passed on to the prototype, in this case her husband, whom she sees as being very much alive and waiting for her in Heaven.

So it is with the veneration of icons. A worshipper enters the Church and approaches an icon. Maybe it's the icon of the saint who is commemorated on that particular day, or of Jesus or the Mother of

God. Making the sign of the cross, followed by a metania, a bow from the waist, the person then kisses the icon, passing on her love and veneration to the prototype it represents. She is *not worshipping the image,* any more than my mother worships a photograph of my father.

SANCTIFYING THE SENSE OF SIGHT

Icons point to beauty and art as a means of experiencing God. In a time when our senses are bombarded with the base things of this world at every turn, now, more than ever, we need for those senses to be sanctified. Saint John of Damascus called sacred images "the books of the illiterate," and asserted that icons sanctify the sense of sight for those who gaze upon them.

Suppose I have few books, or little leisure for reading, but walk into the spiritual hospital—that is to say, a church—with my soul choking from the prickles of thorny thoughts, and thus afflicted I see before me the brilliance of the icon. I am refreshed as if in a verdant meadow, and thus my soul is led to glorify God. I marvel at the martyr's endurance, at the crown he won, and, inflamed with burning zeal, I fall down to worship God through His martyr, and so receive salvation.

If this description of a first century saint's experience seems too removed from our contemporary life, I wonder if that's because we have lost the concept of the Church as a spiritual hospital? Or if, in our fast-paced lives, we have forgotten how to slow down and let the beauty of God's house touch and heal our fragmented psyches.

I have a dear friend from a life-long Protestant Evangelical background who has been visiting my parish for several years. Although she usually goes with her family to their Presbyterian Church on Sundays, she frequents St. John for some of the weekday services. She has told me that, as much as the prayers themselves (usually Third Hour, a short service of Psalms and prayers observed at nine on weekday mornings) bless her, it's the *icons* that are having such a powerful effect on her heart. Sitting alone in the nave after the prayers, gazing at the icon of Christ on the cross—the one the priest carries in procession on Holy Friday—she is sometimes moved to contrition. At other times she feels a longing for a deeper relationship with Christ. She is almost always filled with a sense of His love and peace, on a deeper level—one that transcends emotions. And yes, sometimes her eyes are filled with tears.

Anton Vrame *(The Educating Icon)* would say that my friend has had an *encounter* with icons—that the icon actually *invites a response:* "There is a psychological dimension to the icons in that they sanctify vision, and through it, all bodily senses, pointing to a holistic approach to knowledge and Christian living."

SPIRITUAL SOLEMNITY

So, why doesn't everyone have the same reaction to icons that Saint John of Damascus and Prince Vladimir's men and my friend had? I have another friend who became Orthodox in his seventies, and, as much as he loved and embraced the Orthodox faith, he always struggled with icons. A few years ago I returned home from an iconography workshop at which I had completed an icon of the Holy Apostle Paul. My friend was house-bound, so I was glad to have something other than library books to take with me on one of my visits to his house. But when I showed him the icon, he confessed that he didn't really like looking at them.

"They always look so *sad*," he said. "I thought the Christian life was supposed to be *joyful.*"

I tried to explain that the bright sadness in the faces of the saints depicted in Byzantine icons wasn't like the superficial happiness or romantic beauty found in classical religious art. Icons have a quality which Constantine Cavarnos *(Guide to Byzantine Iconography)* called *hieraticalness* or *spiritual solemnity*. The expressions on the faces of the saints depicted in the icons often reflect the gravity of mankind's circumstances. As Frederica Mathewes-Green says, "No wonder an icon looks so serious. Our condition is serious."

MIRACULOUS AND WEEPING ICONS

Two very mystical examples of God's response to the serious condition of fallen man are miracle-working icons and weeping icons. There are countless stories of people who have been healed by icons, flooding rivers diverted by icons, and cities protected by icons from invaders. Thousands of faithful Christians make pilgrimages to venerate these miraculous icons all over the world. Some are seeking healing; others are offering thanksgiving to God for His protection and grace given through the icon.

My first personal experience with weeping icons happened in 1997. I had the blessing of accompanying several nuns from Holy Dormition Orthodox Monastery in Rives Junction, Michigan to Holy Transfiguration Orthodox Church in Livonia, Michigan, to venerate *four* weeping icons. Each of the icons of the Mother of God had been in the home of a pious woman who brought them to the church as they began to exude myrrh or oil. When these miracles occur, a number of Church hierarchy are called in to verify the legitimacy of the claim. Once confirmed, the icons are usually placed in the church and pilgrims are invited to come and pray before the icons and receive anointing with holy oil from them.

Nothing could have prepared me for this experience. As we entered the church, the nuns were immediately greeted by several parishioners and were invited up to the front of the nave. I followed their examples as they approached each icon, made three prostrations (kneeling and placing their faces on the ground) and then gathered as a group in front of the iconostasis. Then they began to sing hymns to the Mother of God. I tried to sing with them but couldn't stop crying long enough, nor did I want to detract from the celestial purity and beauty of their voices. For me, the spiritual presence of holiness overwhelmed the physical signs—the sweet smell of the myrrh and the visual image of the oil dripping from the icons into containers placed beneath each one. But the physical signs were also indelibly etched into my soul.

A couple of years later I joined three other friends from my parish in Memphis for a weekend pilgrimage to Chicago for the purpose of venerating several miracle-working icons, at three different Orthodox Churches. One of them was the Tikhvin Icon of the Mother of God (attributed to St. Luke), which had been brought to this country from Russia in 1949, to save it from the Communists and Nazis who were destroying icons in Russia. (The Tikhvin Icon was returned to Russia in 2004.)

But it was another miraculous icon, one that has received less attention than the Tikhvin icon, which touched me. Another icon of the Mother of God, it adorned the iconostasis of St. Nicholas Albanian Orthodox Church and began weeping in 1986. What struck me most about our pilgrimage to this particular church wasn't the icon itself. It was the love and devotion expressed by another pilgrim. I didn't talk with this woman, so I don't know her "story." But I watched as she knelt at the back of the nave, and then walked *on her knees* the entire length of the center aisle of the church and crawled up the steps of the solea (the raised platform in front of the iconostasis) to light a candle and venerate this icon. I could hear her praying in another language… and I witnessed a humility and love for God that humbled and inspired me.

BEYOND THE SHATTERED IMAGE

Henri Nouwen was at a retreat in France in 1983 and found that some-one had placed a copy of Rublev's icon of the Trinity on a table in his room. At the same retreat, a year later, an icon of Our Lady of Vladimir was waiting for him. Nouwen entered into a time of spiritual reflection with each icon. The following year, Nouwen added the icons of Christ of Zvenigorod and the Descent of the Holy Spirit (Pentecost) to his experience and wrote a reflection on all four icons, which was published as *Behold the Beauty of the Lord: Praying With Icons.*

Like my friend who struggled with the icon's solemnity, Nouw-en found that icons are "not easy to see." He even called them "rigid, lifeless, schematic and dull" at first. But he gazed at these four icons for hours at a time, and after patient, prayerful stillness on his part, they began to speak to him. As a man who loved the art of Michelange-lo, Rembrandt and Marc Chagall, he could have chosen any of these Western treasures for his meditations. But he chose *icons.* Why?

I have chosen icons because they are created for the sole purpose of offering access, through the gate of the visible, to the mystery of the invisible. Icons are painted to lead us into the inner room of prayer and bring us close to the heart of God.

My favorite section of Nouwen's book is Chapter III—"Seeing Christ." Rublev painted this icon of Christ in the 15th century for a church in the Russian city of Zvenigorod. It was discovered under the steps to a barn in 1918, along with two other famous Rublev icons, where they had been hidden for five centuries.

Nouwen saw, through a prolonged period of prayerful attentiveness to the face of Christ in this damaged image, "a most tender human face, and eyes that penetrate the heart of God as well as every human heart." With further contemplation, he realized that Christ's "sad but still very beautiful face looks at us through the ruins of our world," as if to say, "O what have you done to the work of my hands?"

We are the works of His hands. We are stewards of His world, His creation. Gregory the Theologian refers to the human person as an *icon of God*. John Chryssavgis *(Beyond the Shattered Image)* wrote, "someone who sees the whole world as an icon… has already entered the life of resurrection and eternity. John Climacus, the abbot at St. Catherine's Monastery on Mt. Sinai, was convinced that, in the very beauty and beyond the shattered image of this world:

> … *such a person always perceives everything in the light of the Creator God, and has therefore acquired immortality before the ultimate resurrection."*

As we Christians embrace this iconic way of seeing and living, perhaps we will become better vessels of God's healing.

INCARNATIONAL ART

In the "First Apology of Saint John of Damascus Against Those Who Attack the Divine Images," Saint John talked about Old Testament images like the ark of the covenant (an image of the Holy Virgin and Theotokos) and the rod of Aaron and the jar of manna. These are all visible things that aid understanding of intangible things. We read in Exodus

25-26 how God instructed Moses to use images in the tabernacle—including angels woven on the veil of the holy of holies. It's true that later on God forbade the making of images *because of idolatry*—because of man's misuse of something God intended for good. But that was *before the incarnation,* as St. John explained:

> *It is obvious that when you contemplate God becoming man, then you may depict Him clothed in human form. When the invisible One becomes visible to flesh, you may then draw His likeness. When He who is bodiless and without form, immeasurable in the boundlessness of His own nature, existing in the form of God, empties Himself and takes the form of a servant in substance and in stature and is found in a body of flesh, then you may draw His image and show it to anyone willing to gaze upon it.*

God's incarnation not only made it possible for us to draw and venerate *His* image, but also the images of men and women who have been transfigured by Him—the saints and martyrs. The Seventh Ecumenical Council (787) which upheld the doctrine of the veneration of images as an inevitable result of the incarnation, said this about icons of *saints*:

> *These holy men of all times who pleased God, whose biographies have remained in writing for our benefit and for the purpose of our salvation, have also left to the catholic Church their deeds explained in paintings, so that our mind may remember them, and so that we may be lifted up to the level of their conduct.*

The icons are visions of what we can become if we allow God to penetrate every aspect of our lives. Those who attain this God-likeness to the fullest extent recognized by the Church are *saints*. Their lives, their stories, lift us up to be all that we can be—as we are transformed by God's grace and love.

The Incarnation should cause us to *take our humanity seriously*, as Vrame says. And if we take our humanity seriously, we will not scorn the physical, material things that the Church in Her wisdom has given us as aids for transforming that humanity, for *restoring the image that fell in the beginning*.

The Ethos of Liturgical Art

Taking our humanity seriously also means being concerned about our responsibility to the world around us. Chryssavgis said that our generation is

characterized by a behavior that results from an autism with regard to the natural cosmos: a certain lack of awareness, or recognition, causes us to use, or even waste the beauty of the world…. We have disestablished a continuity between ourselves and the outside, with no possibility for intimate communion and mutual enhancement. The world of the icon, though, restores this relationship by reminding us of what is outside and beyond, what ultimately gives value and vitality.

Like the Incarnation, the icon *pierces space and time*, because a physical object—a piece of wood with gesso and paint and gold leaf—is shot through with God's eternal nature. Christos Yannaras ("The Ethos of Liturgical Art" in *The Freedom of Morality*) said, "Byzantine iconography does not 'decorate' the church but has an organic, liturgical function in the polyphony of the Eucharistic event, existentially elevating us to the hypostatic realization of life." This is heavenly stuff for us mortals to wrap our minds around, but we all need to be elevated—to be lifted up in order to see the world as God sees it—as *sacred* and worthy of redemption.

Chryssavgis also said that the Church as a Eucharistic community "presupposes matter and the use of matter, which is to say *art*, as the creative transformation of matter into a fact of relationship and communion. Man's art, the way he takes up the world and uses it, is a basic element of life, whether it brings about the alienation of life, or makes it incorruptible and raises it to an existential fullness of personal distinctiveness and freedom."

Yes, icons are *art*. They are part of what we offer back to God just as the priest at the altar lifts up the material elements of bread and wine, offering them on behalf of the Eucharistic community—*Thine own of Thine own.* In a mystery, God receives our offering and offers it back to us as the Body and Blood of His Son. And so we offer our *art*—in the form of liturgical music, prayers, architecture, and yes, icons—to the God Who sanctified the world by His incarnation, by becoming man; by becoming matter.

WRITING AND READING: THE GOSPEL IN COLORS

Most iconographers refer to the work they do as *writing* rather than *painting* icons. Just as *hagiography* is the life of a saint written with *words*, *iconography* is the life of the saint written with *paint*. And just as one reads the written life, one also "reads" the painted life—the icon. Again it was the fathers of the Seventh Ecumenical Council who clarified the value of icons as a medium of God's revelation, on a par with the *written* Gospel:

For, when they hear the gospel with the ears, they exclaim "glory to Thee, O Lord"; and when they see it with the eyes, they send forth exactly the same doxology, for we are reminded of his life among men. That which the narrative declares in writing is the same as that which the icon does [in colors].

Following the Council's decree, Patriarch Nicephorus of Constantinople wrote, "If one is worthy of honor, the other is worthy of honor also…. Either accept these [icons], or get rid of those [Gospels]."

The Holy Apostle Luke is perhaps the Church's unique example of one who carried out Christ's great commission in both of these realms—as the writer of the Gospel of Luke, and as the first iconographer. The earliest images of the Mother of God are attributed to him. To this day, iconographers entreat the Holy Apostle Luke, patron saint of iconographers, to guide and bless their work. There is even a special Iconographer's Prayer that commemorates Saint Luke.

WORTH FIGHTING FOR

One of my favorite days of the Church year is the first Sunday of Great Lent, known as "Orthodoxy Sunday." This tradition was established in 842 in Constantinople by His Holiness Patriarch Methodius in memory of the overthrow of the last terrible heresy to rattle the Church, the heresy of iconoclasm. In many cities, the Orthodox faithful from different jurisdictions (Greek, Antiochian, Russian, etc.) join together and worship at one of the larger churches. The children all bring icons, and process with the clergy and altar servers around the inside of the nave at the end of the Liturgy, gathering in front of the iconostasis to face the congregation. The priest reads a proclamation, his voice gaining volume with each line. My heart leaps to join him as he proclaims: "*This* is the Apostolic faith! *This* is the faith of the Fathers! *This* is the Orthodox faith! "

After the priest enumerates some of the wonders of God which are illustrated in the holy icons, the people lift their voices in a song of victory over the iconoclasts:

Who is so great a God as our God?

He is the God who does wonders!

Much ado about… *art?* No wonder the Church celebrates those wise Bishops of the Seventh Ecumenical Council who proclaimed iconography to be an ordinance and tradition which is not something extra, something added to the life of the Church, but, as Chryssavgis says, *a necessary expression of the reality of both God and the world.*

A Life of Partial Virtue
2008

You can't have your cake and eat it, too. If there's one thing Pinkerton's Academy for Young Ladies failed to teach Becky Sharp in William Thackeray's novel, *Vanity Fair*, that was it. Although Thackeray's book was a satire on English society in 1917, some things are just universal—like the endless pursuit of pleasure.

I remember when the first fast-food hamburger place opened in my hometown, Jackson, Mississippi, in the 1950s. Before McDonald's, we had Taylor Burgers, and the first soft-serve ice cream and milkshakes came oozing from those magical machines with the touch of a button. The burgers were mediocre, as I remember, but the French fries—tossed around in hot, oily baskets with a blizzard of salt covering every surface of each morsel—changed a generation of taste buds forever. As hungry Baby Boomers grew up to become successful yuppies, we were easy targets for the Super-Size-It campaign and were quick to agree that we did *deserve a break today*.

Fast food was the gateway drug for this massive group of consumers. By the '60s we had quickly extended our quest for pleasure—drugs, sex and alcohol had failed to put out the fire that seemed to burn brighter with each passing decade. Many of the kids who opted to "turn on, tune in and drop out" in their teens refocused their search inward by their 20s. Eastern religious practices infiltrated the American counter culture and eventually became part of the established spiritual landscape of pleasure-weary pilgrims.

Traditions with Buddhist roots offered the most radical approach to dealing with the abuse of pleasure. One such teaching says that greed, or lust—the Pali term is tanha—binds us to pleasure through the senses, with the result that we become addicted to those pleasures unless we choose to free ourselves from their grip. Either, or. Nothing in between. So when the eye sees something beautiful, or the ear hears a pleasing sound, or the nose smells an enticing aroma, or the tongue tastes a culinary delight, or the body touches something sensual, or even when the mind discovers an intriguing idea, tanha, the strongest bond of desire, takes over our lives, leaving us slaves to our passions.

I was in my mid 40s when I hit the wall, having abused my mind and body with too much of many things. The spiritual path I chose in search for healing wasn't grounded in Buddhism, but in Eastern Orthodox Christian traditions. While I continued (of necessity) to live in "the world" as a wife and mother, I devoted myself to spiritual practices learned from—and more appropriate for—Orthodox monks and nuns. For three years I tried to deny myself pleasures on several fronts, tuning out secular music, literature, television and movies. Taking on a regimen of prayer and fasting designed for those living in monasteries, I set myself up for failure—because I couldn't sustain this level of asceticism. My passions leaked out in numerous ways, and I found myself seeking the same high from spiritual practices that I had once achieved through abuse of food, alcohol and other things. About this time in my life I discovered the famed classic of Russian spirituality: *The Spiritual Life*, by Saint Theophan the Recluse.

Theophan wrote that man has three levels of life—the spiritual, the intellectual and the physical, and that each level has needs. Spiritual needs, he said, are most important, and when they are met in a healthy way, a person will move from that position of peace to meet the needs of the mind and the body, creating harmony of thoughts, feelings, desires and pleasure. Harmony. Balance. That's what I wanted all along—to have my cake and eat it, too.

My search has taken me to exotic places in the pursuit of pleasure, including the beaches of Monaco, Trinidad, Bermuda, Hawaii, and the nearby coasts of Alabama and Florida. I've also fasted and prayed at numerous monasteries and sought enlightenment through pilgrimages to holy places in Greece, England, and even in this country. But it's been my lot to find the beginnings of that elusive balance back home in Memphis, Tennessee, where I no longer beat up on myself when I fail to keep the Orthodox fast perfectly. Or when I skip my morning prayers or drink one too many margaritas. Instead, I take heart from one of Brian Andreas' StoryPeople prints hanging on the wall just above my computer monitor. It's a whimsical stick figure drawing of a woman riding a bicycle, with a basket containing an odd-shaped blue object with several spots on it. The caption says it well:

"She went everywhere with a basket filled daily with a fresh blueberry muffin. It's either that or cigarettes, she said. I am only strong enough for a life of partial virtue."

Burying Saint Joseph
2008

Our house is for sale. During one week in October we touched up the paint on a few walls, bought some plants for the front porch and uncluttered. Well, *somewhat*. You see, the upstairs "landing" is a working art studio, with paints and canvasses and quite a few works in progress. And yes, it tends to be messy. My husband and I share the tiny office downstairs, where we both do lots of writing. And lots of not filing things. And then there's *another* upstairs bedroom into which I dumped boxes of stuff when I cleaned out my mother's house and moved her into an assisted living apartment in 2006. I set up a card table for managing her finances and not filing her paperwork. Real Life is messy.

We have a contingency offer on another house—where we hope to live Real but Less Messy lives—so we handed our keys over to a realtor and left the country (literally) for two weeks.

When we got home, I asked our realtor for feedback from another agent who showed our house. Here's what she said:

Hard to see past all the "icons". (How do you tell people that the stuff that is their business is distracting?)

Yes, I've read the articles about *staging.* I know the philosophy behind getting rid of all your personal stuff so that potential buyers can *see themselves living in your house.* I get all that. And yes, I've found myself distracted, looking at other people's homes and wanting to know more about the people in the family photographs on the walls than about the walls themselves. But I also enjoy absorbing a bit of each home's *ethos...* the human essence that makes it feel like Real People live within its walls.

I also know, from experience, that it often takes twelve to eighteen months to sell a house, and personally, I'm not willing to put my life on hold and live in a museum for that duration.

Which brings me to Saint Joseph. The tradition of burying a statue of Saint Joseph to help sell a home isn't anything new. I'd heard about it over the years, but it wasn't until I began to research staging that I discovered the booming "cottage industry" it has become. There's a book out now, *St. Joseph, My Real Estate Agent: Why the Patron Saint of Home Life is the Patron Saint of Home-Selling.* The author, Stephen J. Binz, includes prayer services for selling a house and claims the practice is not a superstition.

Pope Pius IX proclaimed Joseph the patron of the Universal Church on December 8, 1870. But it's Saint Joseph's life as a husband and father, carpenter and home-builder, that has catapulted him into the spotlight of modern-day real estate. Instructions for burying the Saint Joseph statue often go something like this:

Bury the statue upside down near the For Sale sign in your front yard. Say the following prayer:

> *Joseph of Nazareth,*
> *I beseech thee to intercede on my behalf*
> *To help me find a worthy buyer for my home.*
> *I ask this in the holy name of Christ.*
> *Amen.*

You can even order "Saint Joseph Kits" online, with discounts for realtors who buy in bulk for their clients. The kits come with statues, prayers, the works. Some of these sites include disclaimers from the Catholic Church, whereas others let potential customers draw their own conclusions.

I'm an Eastern Orthodox Christian. Although different jurisdictions of the Orthodox Church (i.e., Greek, Russian, Antiochian)
have tagged some of their saints as patrons of various groups—like
Saint Nicholas for children, sailors and bakers—we don't tend to pray
to them in such exclusive categories. But even if we do seek, for example, St. Phanourios' help in finding a lost object, we don't bury statues
of him in our yards. But we might bake a special St. Phanourios Cake
as a thank offering if the object is found, and give the cake to someone
as a gift.

We paint pictures of saints and we light candles before them
and even kiss them in our personal prayers at home and our corporate
prayers at church. This morning I spent several hours upstairs in my
(messy) studio working on an icon of the Mother of God. It's modeled
after one of the first icons ever painted, by the Apostle Luke. While we
were in Greece (and strangers were walking around in our messy house
back home in Memphis) I saw one of those ancient icons attributed to
Saint Luke. I lit a candle before it in a monastery on the Island of Leros
and asked the intercessions of the Mother of God for a friend who had
just suffered a great loss, and others who are searching for jobs. For one
who is going through a divorce and another who is pregnant. And yes,
for the sale of our house and the purchase of the new one. But after
all of these intercessions I would try to remember to add the following
words, which I learned from a dear Greek friend: *An theli o Theos.* As
God wills. Prayer isn't just about asking for things.

It's not magic. And no, I won't be burying any icons. I also
won't be cleaning up my icon studio and hiding the evidence of the
messy but beautiful lives that are lived here in this house that is for sale.
My husband and I won't stop writing at our computers and leaving
stacks of unfiled paperwork around our crowded but so very Real work-
spaces.

Maybe our house would sell quicker if we buried a Saint Joseph statue or hired a professional stager. Our Realtor has worked with us on and off for almost twenty years. So, my response to her email about the Distracting Icons came as no surprise to her:

"Icons are supposed to be distracting. They're doing their job, distracting people from their earthly lives and pointing them towards spiritual things. They are windows to Heaven."

This place in our home where icons are made, my studio, has been sanctified by their presence. The messy little office has seen the birth of medical articles and essays, short stories and even a novel. Who has time for filing and uncluttering when such creative forces are at work?

Someone will want to live here one day. Someone who knows what a house looks like when it's inhabited by Real People living Real Lives, which are busy and colorful, and sometimes messy.

Finding Balance in Orthodoxy
2012

It is no small thing to leave one's religious upbringing, especially in the South. But my hunger for something different gradually led me away from the Presbyterian faith of my Mississippi childhood.

As a freshman at Ole Miss, I was drawn to Campus Crusade for Christ. When I returned home to Jackson and got married in 1970, I still didn't know what to do with my new enthusiasm for God. I felt like a spiritual orphan. I didn't know where I belonged. I wanted a richer experience of worship and sacramental living.

A group of fellow spiritual expats began gathering in the living room of our apartment. I was a sophomore at Belhaven College, and my husband was a freshman in medical school. We began studying church history, especially the decades prior to the Great Schism (1054). We learned about the Ecumenical Councils, the use of icons, the early liturgy of Saint Justin Martyr, and Saint Ignatius, first bishop of Antioch (consecrated in 69 A.D.).

Eventually, our spiritual search led both my husband and me to the Antiochian Orthodox Church, a branch of the ancient Eastern Orthodox Church. I wrote about our journey in an essay entitled "Chiaroscuro: Shimmer and Shadow," which appears in the new book, *Circling Faith: Southern Women on Spirituality*, just out from the University of Alabama Press.

My husband, William "Bill" Cushman, was ordained an Orthodox priest in the late 1980s. We moved to Memphis, and since 1988 we've been members of Saint John Orthodox Church, where Bill — "Father Basil" — serves as associate pastor. (And yes, he's also a physician).

As often happens when one converts to a new religion, I exhibited radical lifestyle changes for the first ten or so years of my new walk with Jesus in this ancient Christian faith.

Reading mostly monastic literature and emulating the strict ascetic practices found therein, I began wearing a head covering to church, making frequent pilgrimages to monasteries and studying (and eventually teaching) the ancient art of Byzantine iconography.

While all of those practices can certainly be legitimate when done as genuine acts of piety, their presence in my life often reflected a lack of balance. I was rejecting much of what "the world" has to offer in the areas of good secular literature and art. I was trying to find my rhythm in the duality of the spiritual and natural worlds in which I lived.

As the contemporary Russian Orthodox Saint John Maximovitch said: "For all the 'mysticism' of our Orthodox Church that is found in the lives of the Saints and the writings of the Holy Fathers, the truly Orthodox person always has both feet on the ground, facing whatever situation is right in front of him."

By the early 2000s, I began to recover my footing. As I wrote in my essay for *Circling Faith*:

"After about five years of what some of my friends called my 'nun phase,' I took off my head covering and embraced my Southern roots. Manicures, makeup and jewelry returned to my arsenal, and my long-neglected hair again got layered haircuts and blond highlights…. I was asked to speak at a women's retreat hosted by an Orthodox parish in Austin, Texas. I chose as my topic, 'The Middle Way: Finding Balance in Our Lives.' "

Part of that balance, for me, meant being honest about what I wanted to do with my art. I wanted to write novels and study abstract painting, but I was afraid these things weren't acceptable pursuits for a southern church lady.

I met Cassandra King in 2006. Reading her novel *The Sunday Wife* and her essay "The Making of a Preacher's Wife," in the first anthology on Southern women and spirituality, *All Out of Faith*, gave me courage to begin to embrace my true self. Jennifer Horne and Wendy Reed, the editors of both collections of essays, included these words on the inside flap of the first book's cover:

"The South is often considered patriarchal, but as these writers show, Southern culture has always reserved a special place for strong women of passion."

Strong women of passion. I knew I had found soul mates in these new friends.

The Orthodox Church is a spiritual hospital offering sacramental mysteries for the healing of our wounds, but it isn't a panacea for all human ills. I've had my share of dark nights of the soul, and there have been times when I've wanted to leave. But I'm still here, by God's grace, holding my own spiritual feet to the fire and learning to embrace what is real for me.

My essay "Chiaroscuro" ends with these words:

"Maybe my brokenness, like the egg yolks that I use to make tempera paint for my icons — themselves a form of life interrupted — is part of my offering to God."

Holy Mother Mary, Pray to God For Us
2015

It's been a couple of years since I've blogged about my patron saint, Mary of Egypt. But since her feast day is coming up (April 1) and this Sunday is Saint Mary of Egypt Sunday in the Orthodox Church, this seems like a good day for some reflection on her.

About 35 years ago—we had been married for about ten years and were part of a "startup" religious group—my husband returned home from a trip to California he had taken with other "clergy" from our group in Mississippi. They had visited some Orthodox sites and he brought me a gift from one of them—an icon of a scantily-clad saint with sun-bleached skin and hair.

"Who is she?" I asked.

"Her name is Mary of Egypt."

"So, why did you choose this particular icon to bring to me?"

He hesitated a moment, and then said, "She told me to bring it to you."

My husband isn't a touchy-feely sort of guy. At all. He's also not prone to overtly mystical things. Except, of course, that he's an Orthodox priest. But he wasn't a priest when he brought me the icon. He wasn't even sure about her story. So we looked it up and read about her.

It would be another ten years before I would embrace Mary of Egypt as my patron saint. And another ten years before I would come to realize why she reached out to me. But she's been watching over me with diligence for over a quarter of a century now, so I honor her on her two feast days each year. It's a simple gesture, really. I take flowers and place them before her icon at St. John Orthodox Church, my parish here in Memphis. And I continue to ask her to intercede for me in my struggles. That's all.

But that's the once-a-year ritual. The other 364 days each year I simply try to keep her in my heart. Be aware of her presence. Ask for her prayers. Icons help with that. So, at the end of this post I'm going to share a few images of this woman who has come to be known and loved as the "icon of repentance" throughout the Orthodox Church worldwide.

Oh—and I know I've shared this many times, but Mary of Egypt is also featured as one of the three main characters in my novel-in-progress, *Cherry Bomb*. And there are weeping icons (hers) in the book as well.

In April of 1997, when I was visiting an Orthodox monastery in Michigan, I penned the following poem on Saint Mary's Feast Day. Holy Mother Mary, pray to God for us.

Saint Mary of Egypt

Fill my *soul*, O Lord
As you filled the soul of Your Holy Mother;
Let there be no room in my soul
For anything but you.
Fill my *belly*, O Lord
As You filled blessed Mary in the desert;
Let my sustenance be only You
And the blessing of Your Saints.
Fill my *mind*, O Lord
As you filled the theologians
With words to teach us Your ways
And wisdom that gives life.
Fill my *mouth*, O Lord
As you filled the mouth of David,
Enabling him to sing your praise
And teaching repentance through his psalms.
Fill my *days*, O Lord
As you fill each moment of time
With good works appointed for our sake
Increasing us in virtues and piety.
Fill my *nights*, O Lord
As you filled the desert nights
With watchfulness, tears and victory
For holy saints who sought you there.
Fill my *flesh*, O Lord
As you fill those who keep the fast;
With Your own Body and Blood
So that it becomes my only satisfaction.
Fill my *eyes*, O Lord
As once you filled Saint Mary's eyes,
First with humble tears of repentance
And finally with your glorious Light.

A Spiritual Home
2015

A few days ago I received a Facebook message from someone I haven't seen in about forty years. She had recently friended me on Facebook, and I learned that she had moved to the northwest after attending Belhaven College in Jackson, Mississippi, in the early '70s, which is where I knew her. She came to the Bible studies in our apartment in the early gatherings of the group that would eventually become St. Peter Orthodox Church in Jackson.

This person had investigated Orthodoxy but got tripped up in the ritualism, feeling that the "simplicity of Christ" got lost somehow. Eventually she became Catholic (not much ritualism there?) but she's not content. The questions she posed to me in her Facebook message and later in an email were:

Have you found a spiritual home in Orthodoxy?

and

Are you spiritually filled in the Orthodox Church?

I'm glad she asked me both of those questions, because they really are not the same thing at all. My answer to the first question is "Yes." The Orthodox Church is my spiritual home, and has been since 1987 when the group that started out meeting in our apartment in 1970 became an official Orthodox mission and I was Chrismated into the faith. Whether by birth and infant baptism, or by conversion as an adult, when one joins the Orthodox Church it becomes their spiritual home. And the priest and parishioners become their family. Just like one's parents and siblings when one is either born or adopted into a family. It just IS your home.

But that doesn't answer the question I think she was really wanting to ask, which has more to do with how much I like this home. Her second question addresses this issue—are you spiritually *filled* in the Orthodox Church? Interesting choice of a word, *filled*. Again I think of the parallel to my biological family. They fed me, but was I filled? And I think the answer to this question has a lot to do with appetite. What is it you are hungering and thirsting after? Once you decide what you want, then maybe you can determine whether or not your spiritual—or earthly home for that matter—is filling that hunger.

When I am hungering and thirsting after God, the Church satisfies my longing fairly well. I say fairly well because I can't separate my broken human wants and desires from the spiritual thirst that's put there by the Holy Spirit. I don't just want God. I want God… *and* I want (fill in the blank). In my earthly family, I wanted a different kind of mother but I got the mother I got. But our earthly parents are flawed, whereas God is perfect. Perfect love. Perfect wisdom. Perfect grace. I think I just need to want Him more and earthly things less.

This 1000-calorie diet I've been on for a few weeks is teaching me more about what I want. I want to lose weight. But I've got to want that every minute of the day MORE than I want (again fill in the blank) food that isn't good for me or is over my calorie budget. And even when I do the right thing, I don't always get a reward (weight loss). It's a very slow process. Maybe spiritual growth is like that.

So, I tried my best to answer my friend's questions, but my answers aren't necessarily what she needs. She needs to answer those questions for herself—about the Catholic Church (her current spiritual home) or wherever she lands. I sent her a copy of *Circling Faith: Southern Women on Spirituality*, the anthology that has essays by twenty southern women of various faiths, including my essay about my early years as a radical convert to the Orthodox faith. I hope that reading these other women's journeys will help her in her own searching. I don't think one person can tell another which church they should belong to, but I do think that we learn something from being in a family—from living in communion with other human beings.

I also think that some of us—maybe southern women in particular—expect too much from church. I've certainly had my "issues" with my church. When I let go of wanting it to be perfect, I began to be more content. (Maybe another parallel to our earthly families works here, too.) In a way I have freed the Church to be a place I go to worship God and to give something back to Him and to others, rather than I place I go to receive something—a perfect experience of music, theology, art and architecture. The bottom line is it's not perfect and it never will be. But yes, it's my home.

Flannery O'Connor on Writing and (Not) Loving God
2015

A couple of years ago I discovered Flannery O'Connor's wonderful book (published after she died) *A Prayer Journal*. It contains entries she wrote by hand (the hand-written versions are included in the book) from January of 1946 through September of 1947. She was only twenty-one when she began this short journal. For some reason I was drawn back to this journal this morning and began reading it again with my second cup of coffee. I hear my own thoughts—my own voice—in so many of her words. It blesses me to see a (southern) writer of O'Connor's talent express her struggle with faith. I'll share a few excerpts, beginning with the final entry in the journal, because I have experienced such similar feelings recently:

> *My thoughts are so far away from God. He might as well not have made me. And the feeling I end up writing here lasts approximately a half hour and seems a sham. I don't want any of this artificial superficial feeling stimulated by the choir. Today I have proved myself a glutton—for Scotch oatmeal cookies and erotic thought. There is nothing left to say of me.*

When I first read this I thought someone had been listening in on my confessions! Just replace scotch oatmeal cookies with homemade fudge (the object of my gluttony last week) and the rest fits. A priest once asked me—after giving me absolution after my confession—"Do you love God?" I answered that I must not, or else I would behave differently. But I WANT TO love God, so that's a start. Again O'Connor's words bless me:

> Dear God, I cannot love Thee the way I want to. You are the slim crescent of a moon that I see and myself is the earth's shadow that keeps me from seeing all the moon. The crescent is very beautiful and perhaps that is all one like I am should or could see; but what I am afraid of, dear God, is that my self shadow will grow so large that it blocks the whole moon, and that I will judge myself by the shadow that is nothing. I do not know you God because I am in the way. Please help me to push myself aside.

Reading her words here makes me wonder if I struggle with loving God because I love myself too much. Or I am too much concerned with my work, with my success. I am heartened that O'Connor expresses this same concern several times in her journal:

> I want very much to succeed in the world with what I want to do....
> Please help me dear God to be a good writer and to get something else accepted....
> Oh dear God I want to write a novel, a good novel. I want to do this for a good feeling & for a bad one. The bad one is uppermost. The psychologists say it is the natural one....

But later (is she making spiritual "progress"?) she says:

> *I want so to love God all the way. At the same time I want all the things that seem opposed to it—I want to be a fine writer. Any success will tend to swell my head—unconsciously even. If I ever do get to be a fine writer, it will not be because I am a fine writer but because God has given me credit for a few of the things He kindly wrote for me.*

So there it is—the dichotomy I face every day. But perhaps also a way to face it, by acknowledging God's gifts to me. And by continuing to ask God to help me love Him, as O'Connor entreated Him:

> *Dear Lord please make me want You. It would be the greatest bliss…. Give me the grace, dear God, to adore You, for even this I cannot do for myself.*

Pilgrim Interrupted

I was in the Cave of the Apocalypse on the Island of Patmos, Greece on October 21, 2007. It was the Feast Day of Saint Christodolous, who founded the Monastery of the Holy Apostle John in 1088. Aside from the sense of awe one would expect to feel in such a sacred place, my emotions were pretty much intact—until, well, let me set this up for you first.

The evening before, we had joined the large crowd of pilgrims at the main church of the monastery for Vigil, a three to four hour service on the eve of a feast. The music was powerful. At one point, all the monks came out from the altar area and other places throughout the church and formed a semi-circle in front of the abbot. Their voices swelled to the top of this ancient church, resounding off the towering iconographic images that filled the walls and even the dome. A huge chandelier, lit by dozens of beeswax candles, reflected back the gold leaf of the halos surrounding us.

I felt like Prince Vladimir's envoys when they walked into Hagia Sophia Orthodox Cathedral in Constantinople near the end of the tenth century. Their mission was to find a religion that Prince Vladimir could embrace and offer to the people of Russia. In their report they said, "We didn't know whether we were in Heaven or on earth."

Heavenly as it was, we chose to attend church in the Cave of the Apocalypse the following morning rather than returning to the "big" church. We were drawn to the intimacy and history of this place where the Holy Apostle John had heard the voice of God speak to him the words that would become known as the Book of Revelation.

My husband is an Orthodox priest. We were traveling with another priest and his wife, old friends from Mississippi. Arriving at the tiny church inside the cave, I was surprised to see that the only other worshippers were two men and a young boy at the chanter's stand, and Father Seraphim, the monk-priest who had been assigned to serve in the cave. A few minutes later, a woman came in and sat on the bench near my friend and me, and a small family arrived and stood in the back. So there we were, a congregation of nine lay persons and three priests, inside one of the most sacred places in all of Orthodoxy, or Christendom, for that matter.

And then everything changed. The altar boy, who had been multi-tasking as chanter, sub-deacon, and interpreter between Father Seraphim (who spoke no English) and our priest husbands (who spoke little Greek), suddenly greeted a blond woman wearing a name tag and holding a clipboard. They whispered briefly, and then the woman motioned towards the entrance to the cave and in they came, droves— I mean *droves*— of tourists, fresh off the cruise boat docked at the bottom of the hill.

It was surreal— like an invasion of the profane into the sacred— and it continued for about forty-five minutes. They would enter to the right of us, in their khaki shorts, fanny packs, and white Keds and cameras (which weren't allowed inside the cave) and move slowly along the wall where Saint John had once sat, dictating to his scribe, Prochorus. The tour guide alternately pointed to the hole in the wall where the disciple pulled himself up after sitting for hours on end, and the crack in the ceiling where he heard the voice of God. Their mouths formed large, silent "Os" as they crept along, nodding at one another. Then the guide would wave the tourists through the tiny chapel, and they would walk in front of us as they exited.

To say it was a distraction would be a huge understatement. I could hardly stop watching the stream of visitors who found themselves in the middle of the Divine Liturgy of the Orthodox Church, thinking they were simply touring an historic site. They stared at our husbands, who were wearing traditional Greek skoufi (hats) and black cassocks, and sometimes at my friend and me, as we crossed ourselves and bowed during certain parts of the service. Every now and then one of them would stop and sit down on one of the benches, to catch their breath, or maybe even to pray, only to be hurried along by the tour guide like a kindergarten teacher correcting an errant child.

How strange, I thought, that they would schedule tours during the church services, when they could as easily wait until later in the morning or in the afternoon. And then I noticed that the priest, chanters and altar server didn't seem a bit disturbed. They were used to it, I'm sure, but I wondered if they weren't also tuned in to the bigger picture: the cave is not a museum. It's a tabernacle of the living God, serving up the Holy Mysteries to a smattering of worshippers who faithfully pray in a church that also happens to be a major tourist attraction.

After the service, we were invited for refreshments in Father Seraphim's apartment. We were served strong Greek coffee and warm fellowship by this humble gathering of people whose love extends to pilgrim and tourist alike. It was there that the words of Saint John finally hit me: "Little children, love one another." *Even the tourists.*

(Jesus Said the) Boys *(Could be)* in Charge

"I *know* Jesus said the boys could be in charge." This simple admission was made by my friend on a beautiful March afternoon at the beach, of all places. The location really has no significance to the topic, other than giving you, the reader, a visual image of the venue for this particular discussion. I say *particular* because discussions of this nature are nothing new for my friend and me. Over the years we've held court at coffee shops, bars, monasteries, women's retreats, each other's homes, fishing camps, and hotel rooms we rented when we were too tired to keep driving on one of our road trips together. And yes, we've also logged lots of hours on our cell phones and written endless emails when we were back in our separates homes in Tennessee and Arkansas.

It's important to say up front that we are *not* feminists. Not even *close*. In fact, we're both converts to the ancient Orthodox Christian Church—the one established by Jesus Himself in 33 A.D. on the day of Pentecost. That was when God the Father sent God the Holy Spirit to comfort, guide and teach the early Christians how to set up the Church on Earth and how to *live*. A few days earlier Jesus had told His disciples *and the women who were with them* that He couldn't stay with them on Earth any longer–but it was time for Him to *go to the Father*. So he ascended to Heaven. And yes, *He said the boys could be in charge*.

He said the boys could be in charge, even though it was the girls, and especially the myrrhbearing women, who weren't afraid to go to His tomb to honor Him, putting their lives in danger by this courageous act of love and devotion. Where were the boys when He appeared to Mary Magdalen and the other women?

He said the boys could be in charge, even though it was a "sinful woman" who taught the boys a lesson in financial management when she used expensive perfume to anoint Jesus' feet. When the boys, especially Judas, complained about this "frivolous" use of the gang's money, Jesus put them in their place. For the time being.

He said the boys could be in charge, even though Judas stole and Paul persecuted and Thomas doubted and Peter denied and all of them fell asleep when Jesus needed them most, at Gethsemane.

He said the boys could be in charge, even though husbands and brothers and fathers and even grandfathers have used their authority to intimidate young granddaughters and daughters and sisters and wives into silent submission during countless acts of sexual, physical and emotional abuse.

He said the boys could be in charge, even though there have been throughout history, and continue to be, narcissistic, abusive men in the ranks of our clergy. And evil, self-serving men as leaders of kingdoms and nations. And even patriarchal good-old-boys who aren't really *bad*, but who perpetuate a chauvinistic oppression that affects even healthy church communities.

None of this is to take away from the lives of true repentance and self-sacrifice and faith and miracle-working that Jesus' disciples eventually lived. *Men of whom the world was not worthy*. Men who became saints . . . whose icons adorn our churches, many of whom are chosen as patrons for churches and monasteries all over the world. As an iconographer, I have painted the images of some of those Holy men, including John, Paul, Andrew, Basil the Great, Emperor Constantine, Macarius the Great, Nicholas, Seraphim of Sarov, and John the Baptist. I love these men and venerate their holy icons and ask their intercessions on a daily basis.

But I also have painted icons of the Mother of God, Mary Magdalen, Mary of Egypt, Catherine the Great, Perpetua, Zenobia, and Juliana the Merciful. Admittedly, my limited experience of the communion of the saints has been greater with these Holy women than with the Holy men mentioned above. Maybe that's only natural–like calls out to like. And I must say that each of them helps me accept, as they did, Jesus' decision to let the boys be in charge.

Juliana the Merciful, also known as Juliana "the housewife," lived in Moscow in the sixteenth century. She was orphaned at six, when her parents died, and again at twelve, when her grandmother died. At sixteen she married "up," as we say in the South. Her wealthy in-laws resented her, forcing her to work twice as hard to win their approval. Before and after her early widowhood, she did works of mercy–she fed the poor, nursed the sick, visited those in prison, buried the dead. She could have wasted her energy being angry at her husband's condescending family and complaining that the boys were in charge. Instead, she responded to God's love and blessings in her life with humility and acts of love and mercy. She is portrayed in her icon holding, of all things, *a cleaning cloth*, near her face, offering it up to God as one full of gratitude.

Catherine the Great debated with 150 rhetoricians brought forth by the Emperor Maximus and ended up converting them all before the emperor condemned them to death by fire for embarrassing him by losing to a woman. The emperor's wife visited Catherine in prison, and he had her beheaded. When Catherine refused to become his queen, he had her beheaded, as well, at the age of eighteen, in the early fourth century. I wonder if Catherine ever questioned why Jesus said the boys could be in charge.

Perpetua was martyred in Carthage in 202 A.D. after spending time in prison, separated from her nursing baby. Zenobia was watching her brother, a physician who was being tortured by the order of the Emperor Diocletian, when she cried out, "I'm a Christian, too" and joined him in his martyrdom in Cilicia in the third century. Mary of Egypt was a fifth century prostitute who was refused entry into a church in Jerusalem to venerate the true cross. When I first read her story, I thought, "how judgmental… like she's the only sinful person who goes to church!" Later, when I got to know her and learned of her repentance and years of asceticism and solitude in the wilderness, and the miracles she performed there and the impact she had on the priest, Zosimos, I embraced her humility and took her as my patron saint.

And then there are the other Marys. Mary Magdalen, the Myrrhbearer, is also known as "Equal-to-the-Apostles." Not that she cared about titles. She only cared about the fact that Jesus healed her of evil spirits and changed her life forever. She stood bravely with the *other* Mary, the Mother of God, at the crucifixion, and later traveled to Rome and urged Caesar to exile Pilate to Gaul, which he did. She aided John the Theologian in his missionary work and taught the Gospel. She never seemed to mind that Jesus said the boys could be in charge. But then, again, look who she hung out with–the cream of the crop.

Mary the Mother of God is the one that stops me in my tracks. I truly believe that there are numerous well-known, well-written, feminist authors around today–some of whom I read with guarded relish–whose angry fires would be quenched, or at least subdued, if they knew *Her*. She understood the deal from the beginning, when she volunteered to live as a virgin in the temple at age three, being fed by angels. She understood when Archangel Gabriel told her the plan—that the whole world was counting on her response: "Be it done unto me according to Thy will." She understood at the wedding in Cana when they ran out of wine and she approached Her Son about the problem and He seemed to dismiss her, saying, "Woman, what does your concern have to do with Me?" She knew that the boys were in charge, so she said to the servants, "Whatever He says to you, do it." And He worked his first miracle, turning the pots of water into wine. I've often wondered why He chose such a seemingly insignificant situation for His first miracle—a simple matter of inadequate refreshments at a wedding—rather than raising someone from the dead, as He did later in His ministry. Wedding receptions and feasts and showers and luncheons and dinner parties are usually situations in which the girls are in charge, aren't they? Unless there is something subtle at work here that we're missing. Something about Jesus being in charge . . . being the "unseen guest at every table" and all that sort of thing.

So, if we learn our lessons well, men, women, and children will all come to understand that, however it plays out in our institutions and ceremonies, *Jesus is really in charge.* It's His image that the priest represents to us when he stands at the altar preparing the gifts for the sacrament of Holy Communion. It's His image that the confessor represents to us as we stand beside him at the sacrament of Confession. It's His image that the deacons and altar *boys* represent to us as they serve in Holy Liturgy. And yes, the image is tarnished. The Church is not perfect. But whose fault is that? Is it because He said the boys could be in charge?

Look at the place He gave His Mother. All generations call Her blessed. Her icon adorns every iconostasis. Many feasts of the Church are dedicated to Her. I find it really hard to remain angry when standing before the icon of the Mother of God, Directress—the one in which She is directing our gaze to Her Son. *Do what He tells you.* Simple. Direct. It's like She knows we need His masculine strength, along with Her feminine courage and endurance. When Mary of Egypt couldn't get a foot in the door at the Church in Jerusalem, she fell on her knees before the icon of the Mother of God on the outside wall of the church and begged for entrance. The Mother of God granted her entrance. Where did she get that power? That authority? Maybe it was because she was content that *Jesus said the boys could be in charge.*

The Imperfect Peace
2009

O'Connor said it was Christ-haunted,
My home, the South.
Maybe that's why
I can't escape His hold on me,
Like Jacob, who wrestled with the angel.

Sometimes I want to run away,
From my roots,
From my God,
But neither will let me go,
And for that I am, at long last, grateful.

The angry child tries to escape
His father's embrace,
And fights against
His mother's love
Until, exhausted, he collapses in her bosom.

That's where I find myself today,
At rest in the arms
Of Christ and the South,
Having at long last
Buried the sword and accepted the imperfect peace.

II

WRITING, EDITING, AND PUBLISHING

Writing isn't about making money, getting famous, getting dates, getting laid, or making friends. In the end, it's about enriching the lives of those who will read your work, and enriching your own life, as well…. Writing is magic, as much the water of life as any other creative art. The water is free. So drink. Drink and be filled up.

—Stephen King, *On Writing*

There's no greater agony than bearing an untold story inside you.—*Maya Angelou*

I want very much to succeed in the world with what I want to do…. Please help me dear God to be a good writer and to get something else accepted…. Oh dear God I want to write a novel, a good novel. I want to do this for a good feeling & for a bad one. The bad one is uppermost. The psychologists say it is the natural one.

—Flannery O'Connor *(A Prayer Journal)*

Writing Memoir: Art vs. Confessional
2011

A couple of years ago, during a manuscript critique workshop I was attending in Oxford, Mississippi, workshop leader Scott Morris (*Waiting for April, The Total View of Taftly*) said something I will never forget:

> *A memoir must be artful and not just real. Yes, you've lived it—the abuse, the loss, the suffering—now you have to get up and above it, distance yourself, and spin a good yarn. You've got to create art from what you lived.*

It's not that he was being insensitive to the painful stories that were so courageously shared by the new writers at the workshop—he genuinely cared about what we had lived through. But he wasn't there in the role of therapist. He was there to help us become better writers. "We write to reclaim a part of our life," he said, "but it has to be about the art."

There are plenty of opportunities to talk about the trauma in your life, if that's what you want to do. If you're into public confession, you can get paid to air your dirty laundry on talk shows. If it's healing you're after, there are the traditional and private venues like the psychologist's office and the church confessional. If you believe you just have to write about what happened to you, go ahead.

But don't try to get it published, unless you do the hard work of spinning that painful experience into the golden threads of an artful memoir.

My favorite memoirists have all done this well: Mary Karr has mined a rough childhood for three brilliantly written volumes: *The Liar's Club*, *Cherry* and *Lit*. Augusten Burroughs has carried his horrific story through nearly a half dozen books. Haven Kimmel's *A Girl Named Zippy* and *She Got Up Off the Couch* were anything but sappy confessionals. And Kim Michelle Richardson's heartbreaking story of abuse at the hands of priests and nuns at the Catholic orphanage where she grew up—*The Unbreakable Child*—reads more like a novel than a revenge piece. (Although her attorney has certainly called Rome into account.)

In November I was down in Oxford (Mississippi) again—this time as co-director of the 2010 Creative Nonfiction Conference—when I was treated to yet another unveiling of a memoir masterpiece.

I hadn't even read his work yet when I introduced Robert Goolrick as one of the panelists for our afternoon session. He was going to be signing and reading from his memoir *The End of the World As We Know It* later that evening at Off Square Books.

I had no idea what I was in for. I sat near the front so that I could take pictures for my blog, but I almost had to leave before it was over, for fear of disturbing the others who had come to hear him. You see, I was bawling during most of his reading. People were passing me tissues. A new acquaintance put her arm around me supportively.

Goolrick was raped by his father "just once" when he was a small boy and his father was drunk. His memoir describes, in the most powerful, dark, poetic prose I've ever read on the subject, the ongoing effects on the soul of the person who is violated in this way:

> *If you don't receive love from the ones who are meant to love you, you will never stop looking for it, like an amputee who never stops missing his leg, like the ex-smoker who wants a cigarette after lunch fifteen years later. It sounds trite. It's true. You will*

*look for it in objects that you buy without want. You will look for
it in faces you do not desire. You will look for it in expensive hotel
rooms, in the careful attentiveness of the men and women who
change the sheets every day, who bring you pots of tea and thinly
sliced lemon and treat you with false deference....
You will look for it in shop girls and the kind of sad and splendid
men who sell you clothing. You will look for it and you will never
find it. You will not find a trace.*

If you haven't guessed by now, I was sexually abused. First,
by my grandfather when I was a young girl. And later by others in my
young adult life. And yes, I've spent many hours talking with therapists
and priests and other victims of abuse, and no, *I'm not okay.* If Goolrick
is right, I may never be okay.

And yet I found it darkly comforting, listening to him read these
words that explain why he decided to tell his story:

*I tell it because there is an ache in my heart for the imagined
beauty of a life I haven't had, from which I have been locked out,
and it never goes away.*

Writing his memoir didn't heal Goolrick's pain, but he certainly
did "get up and above it" and what he wrote is art of the highest caliber.

My writing critique group will probably be the only people ever
to read all eighteen chapters of the memoir I spent two years writing.
Just as it was beginning to vaguely resemble art, I realized I wasn't willing to go public with it, and so I abandoned it for fiction. Maybe there,
in the writing of a novel, I can find "the imagined beauty of a life I
haven't had."

Living With a Writer's Brokenness
2011

I recently read *The Paris Wife* by Paula McLain. It's a novel about Ernest Hemingway's first marriage, to Hadley Richardson, written through her voice. I thought I'd share some of it as part of my post here on what it's like to be married to a writer.

Ernest and Hadley were married during the time he lived in Paris and wrote *The Sun Also Rises*, which fictionalizes quite a bit of their hard-drinking fast-living life with a colorful circle of friends in Paris. It was Hadley's lot to be his wife during his early years of struggling to find his voice as a writer, as she struggled to hold onto herself as a woman while being his wife and muse. This sentence shows some of Hadley's struggle:

"I close my eyes and lean into Ernest, smelling bourbon and soap, tobacco and damp cotton—and everything about this moment is so sharp and lovely, I do something completely out of character and just let myself have it."

Why was it out of character for Hadley to let herself have that lovely and intimate moment with him? I think she took her role as muse and supporter to a brilliant artist more seriously than her role as his lover and wife, so she devalued herself as a person. McLain creates lots of dialogue that shows this aspect of their relationship:

"I'm not sure I get it completely, but I can tell you're a writer. Whatever that thing is, you have it." *(Hadley)*

"God that's good to hear. Sometimes I think all I really need is one person telling me that I'm not knocking my fool head against the bricks. That I have a shot at it." *(Ernest)*

And then she shows the complexity of their relationship through interior monologue: *(Hadley thinking)*

> *... it struck me how comfortable I felt with him, as if we were old friends or had already done this many times over, him handing me pages with his heart on his sleeve—he couldn't pretend this work didn't mean everything to him—me reading his words, quietly amazed by what he could do. . . .*

And the limitations that Ernest's work put on the marriage: *(again through Hadley's thoughts)*

> *Hadn't I just felt us collapsing into one another, until there was no difference between us? It would be the hardest lesson of my marriage, discovering the flaw in this thinking. I couldn't reach into every part of Ernest and he didn't want me to. He needed me to make him feel safe and backed up, yes, the same way I needed him. But he also liked that he could disappear into his work, away from me. And return when he wanted to.*

I have to get away from my home, and from my husband (whom I love) in order to get serious amounts of writing done, which is why I spent the month of November writing at the beach. And sometimes I just need hours of quiet to think, before ever putting words on the page. I found it interesting that Hemingway also felt that way, and Hadley wished he wouldn't leave:

> *"It's been so long since you've even tried to write here at home. Maybe it would work now and I could see you. I wouldn't have*

to talk or disturb you." (Hadley)
"You know I need to go away to make anything happen…. I
have to be alone to get it started…." (Ernest)

A couple of weeks ago I went to the Yoknapatawpha Summer Writers Workshop in Oxford, Mississippi. One night the workshop leader, Scott Morris, gave his annual craft talk, this time on "Voice." One thing that stuck with me long after his talk was what he said about the writer's cross—that we will always be reaching for something just beyond our grasp, using words to make sense of the world and to make peace with our suffering:

"The novel will just sit down in that place of suffering and spend time there…. The great novel trades in regret…. This type of writing is up against the dominant culture of the day…. Great writing is about going to those wounds and staying there."

This reminded me of something Hadley thought about Ernest later in the novel:

It gave me a sharp kind of sadness to think that no matter how much I loved him and tried to put him back together again, he might stay broken forever…. He wanted everything there was to have and more than that.

We are all broken creatures, but I think that artists and writers carry our brokenness in a more intense manner. It's hard on our families. Although my husband is also a writer, he's a physician (and a priest) and most of his writing is scientific. He has no problem writing an article for the *New England Journal of Medicine* while I'm in the room with him (and a football game is on television and he's checking email

on his Blackberry). But I need physical and emotional space in order
to create words on the page, and he gets that. Our kids have been out
of the house for ten years now, and we celebrated our 41st wedding anniversary on June 13, so he's been living with my brokenness for quite
some time. But unlike Hadley and Ernest, we're not "collapsing into
one another." We're two fully realized persons who don't need the other
person to complete us. Instead, we are learning to be supportive of each
other's careers, which we are both passionate about. Hopefully we've
dodged the bullet that destroyed Ernest and Hadley's marriage, which
McLain describes in the Epilogue of the book, thirty-five years after
their divorce, when they are both married to other people:

> *"Tell me, do you think we wanted too much from each other? . .*
> *. . Maybe that's it. We were too hooked into each other. We loved*
> *each other too much." (Ernest)*
> *"Can you love someone too much?" (Hadley)*

He was quiet for a moment. "No," he finally said, his voice very
soft and sober. "That's not it at all. I ruined it."

Hard Labor: The Birth of a Novelist
2018

In October 2006 I met five women who would unwittingly become instigators in the long, laborious process of my birthing as a novelist. Lee Smith, Cassandra King, Beth Ann Fennelly, Jennifer Horne, and Wendy Reed were speaking at the Southern Festival of Books the last year the festival was hosted by Memphis. (Nashville has hosted the annual event since then.) Lee was giving a talk about her latest book, *On Agate Hill*, and I instantly became a fan. Although we didn't have much time to talk personally, I was drawn to her voice, and I was inspired by her longevity—she had written and published ten novels over a period of forty years. Beth Ann had a nonfiction book out, *Great with Child*, but I was mesmerized by her poetry collection, *Tender Hooks*, and like most people when they first meet Beth Ann, I had a huge girl crush. She had on snug jeans with tall boots, and her beautiful auburn hair hung halfway down her back in sexy waves. Jennifer and Wendy were on a panel discussing an anthology they co-edited, *All Out of Faith: Southern Women on Spirituality*, which made me want to run home and pen an essay immediately.

But my most vivid memory from the weekend is a conversation I had with Cassandra as she signed a copy of her latest novel, *The Sunday Wife*. Our stories were similar, in that we both were married to ministers and spent years doing the "expected thing" with our art—creating religious pieces for the church newsletter or bulletin and writing children's Christmas plays. It wasn't until she shared her Truth (capital T intentional) with me—that she had always wanted to write novels— that we embraced, and she signed my copy of her book, "To Susan, who knows what a Sunday Wife is." A seed was planted, and hope was springing up in me. Could I become a novelist? I fell in love with each of these women for different reasons, but they all inspired me, as did the novelist Joshilyn Jackson, whom I had met the previous summer at the first annual Mississippi Writers Guild Conference. Best-selling short story author John Floyd critiqued my less-than-wonderful attempt at writing short fiction, and I knew then I needed the longer narrative form to tell a decent story. Since I'm originally from Jackson, Mississippi, it was a joy to share a weekend with established and up-and-coming writers from my home state, and I found myself singing along with Rodney Atkins's song "These Are My People" on the radio as I drove back to Memphis.

Over the next few months I wrote my first novel, *The Sweet Carolines*, in a coffee shop. It remains in a box on a shelf, but some of its characters and plot lines emerged as incarnations in my later work. Struggling with fiction, I took to writing essays and was happy to find publishing homes for a dozen or more of them over the next ten years. As Anne Lamott says, the essay is so much easier to write than the novel—it's more like a one-night stand, whereas writing a novel is more like a marriage. But since I've been married forty-seven years, I should have acquired the patience and perseverance to write a book-length story, right?

Next I tried my hand at memoir, as much for therapy as art. But eventually I realized that I wasn't willing to go public with some of the names that peopled my stories of childhood and young adulthood sexual abuse and unhappiness in the cult-like religious group in which I spent almost two decades of my life. One of my mentors, the author Scott Morris, critiqued my early chapters of the memoir at the Yoknapatawpha Summer Writers Workshops (a.k.a. the YOK Shop) I attended in Oxford, Mississippi, several summers between 2007 and

2015. He taught me that if I was going to write "confessional prose," I needed to learn to get up and above the pain and make *art*. It was then that I realized I should try fiction again.

In 2010 and 2011, I drafted a new novel, *Cherry Bomb*. Scott and my fellow participants at the YOK Shop critiqued early drafts of *Cherry Bomb*, and the first three chapters made the short list in the "Novel-in-Progress" category of the 2011 Faulkner-Wisdom Creative Writing Competition. In 2012 I hired a freelance editor and enlisted several "early readers"—and the members of the writing group I was in at the time—to give feedback on the manuscript and help me polish the book. Next I spent six months querying seventy-five literary agents. About twenty-five of them asked to read the full manuscript, and many wrote really nice rejection letters. Finally agent number seventy-five *loved* the book. She asked if she could send it to an editor for an overview (at a cost of $750) and I didn't know any better than to say yes.

For the next two years (with a three-month interruption when I was in a car wreck and couldn't work) I worked with this agent, even meeting with her in person in New York City, and she continued to tell me she loved the book. But she also continued to convince me to send it to yet another editor (for another $750) as it wasn't quite "up to commercial standards" yet. This process was extremely frustrating, as these editors often gave me contradictory advice. The book has three main characters. One editor encouraged me to completely delete one of the characters (and the three chapters written in her voice) while another editor declared that character to be her favorite in the book. One editor encouraged me to read *The Girl with the Dragon Tattoo* and to make my protagonist more "hard ass"—like Lisbeth Salander—while another asked me to rewrite the entire manuscript, changing it from present tense to past tense. As I shared my struggles with several friends who were published authors, each of them expressed concerns about the agent charging me for editing. When she asked me if she could send it out for a fourth major revision, I parted ways with her. That was one of the hardest things I have ever done.

I spent the next few months querying agents again, and after another fifty (yes) rejections, I finally made the decision to give up on my dream for a book deal with one of the big publishing houses. I began querying small presses that don't require agent representation, and finally, in November 2016, I signed a contract with a small press in Mississippi. *Cherry Bomb*—a novel about a graffiti writer, an abstract expressionist painter, and a nun, set mostly in Georgia—had found a home and would be published in August 2017. The editing process was so much better this time. Collaborating with the publisher, going through the manuscript chapter by chapter, we partnered to kill a few darlings and to birth a few more, lifting the narrative arc in places where it sagged and inserting scenes where more were needed. Working with a small press gave me a sense of ownership in my work. I was even invited to give input on the cover design, which was important to me as an artist. What I gave up (money? fame?) by not having an agent and a book deal with one of the big five, I gained in the joy of intimate involvement in every step of the publishing process.

So, in a sense, the birthing of my first novel was a ten-year labor of love. Along the way I often wondered if I have what it takes to be a novelist. I took some "detours," writing and publishing a nonfiction book about caregiving for my mother, who died of Alzheimer's in May 2016. *Tangles and Plaques: A Mother and Daughter Face Alzheimer's* was culled from sixty blog posts covering over eight years of Mother's decline. Back at that Mississippi Writers Guild Conference in 2006, Joshilyn Jackson had encouraged me to start a blog in order to build a platform and grow an audience of readers. Little did I know then that a decade later (posting religiously three times a week about topics like mental health, art, religion, writing, and literature) sixty of those posts would find new life as essays in a book.

Other detours included contributing essays to three anthologies. In all three cases, my experience working with the editors of these anthologies was positive. I came to realize how much I loved the genre, and decided to try and edit one myself.

A Second Blooming: Becoming the Women We Are Meant to Be was my first collection to organize and edit. I was through-the-roof with excitement as twenty excellent writers agreed to contribute (I even got a foreword by Anne Lamott) and Mercer University Press offered to publish the book. I began to think that I enjoy editing more than writing. And I've always loved to organize things—like the literary salons I host in our home here in Memphis several times a year—so grouping the essays by themes and finding quotes to anchor each section was simply fun. It was such a nice break from the labor-intensive writing and revising involved with the novel. I was so exhausted from the six years involved in the production of *Cherry Bomb* that I declared (as I'm sure many mothers have done post-partum) never to write another novel. But—also like those new mothers—it wasn't long before my mind began to long for another child and to dream up new characters and new locations and new plot lines. By the time this collection goes to press, I hope to have another novel in the oven. Yes, the pain of childbirth passes, and the possibility of bringing something literary, something hopefully wonderful, into the world is great enough to endure another pregnancy. In a sense, this essay is a thank-you letter to my early lovers—the ones who planted those first seeds—because I truly believe I would not have become a writer without them. But it's also a nod to future midwives whom I look forward to working with as the labor continues.

Friends of the Library

Without libraries what have we? We have no past and no future.—Ray Bradbury

In a previous essay in this collection, I wrote about the four book deals I got in one year for my first four books, which were published in 2017 and 2018. And yes, two of those books had been in the works for many years, but a couple of them came together fairly quickly. As did my fifth book, *Friends of the Library*. Let me tell you its story.

My publisher for *Cherry Bomb*, my novel, sent me on a book tour to numerous "Friends of the Library" groups in small towns in Mississippi, mostly in 2017. Although I had grown up in Jackson, and had attended the University of Mississippi in Oxford, I had not visited most of these small towns in my home state. Towns like Eupora, Aberdeen, Senatobia, Southaven, Starkville, West Point, and Pontotoc. I had spent a good bit of my childhood in my mother's hometown, Meridian, where my grandparents lived. And I had visited Vicksburg a few times when I lived in Jackson. But I was fascinated to learn the histories of all these Mississippi towns, and to drive through their neighborhoods filled with historic homes and their quaint downtown settings. *Settings*. That's exactly what they became. Settings for a collection of short stories, which I published in 2019. I actually wrote a couple of blog posts about those library visits, which I looked at later when the idea for the short stories came to mind. And while *Friends of the Library* gives its readers plenty of factual information about each town—including its history and certain aspects of its culture—the characters and their stories are completely fictional.

It was fun writing those stories through the eyes of the fictional author Adele Covington, who traveled from her home in Memphis to speak at these libraries. Oh, and I love giving some of my characters names that connect back to me or something in my life. Adele's first name came from my middle name, Dell. And Covington was my grandmother's maiden name. It's fun to sneak those connections into my fiction. (I did the same with a few of the unsavory characters in *Cherry Bomb*, so I won't call them out now.)

I'm not sure who inspired the character Odell McPherson, the homeless man in Webster County who shows up at the Friends' monthly meetings unwashed, unkempt, and quoting Wendell Berry. Maybe it's the homeless people I've met frequently in Memphis, especially during the twenty-five years we lived in midtown. I remember one really cold winter when I cooked beef stew and gave it out on our front porch to a number of people who wandered our neighborhood begging alms. And the bottles of cold water I loaded into ice chests in the back of my car during the hottest summer days and gave out with snacks at various spots where homeless people gather downtown. It just came natural that Adele would want to help Odell (Oh, wow, I actually just now noticed that Odell's name also has "Dell" in it!), and so she comes up with a plan. She involves Miss Francine Pittman—an elderly woman who lives in the beautiful but derelict Victorian home across the street from the library—in her plan, which ends up helping both of them. Did I mention that Francine went to college with Eudora Welty and wanted to be a writer when she was younger? You'll have to read the story to find out how that worked out.

The story I set in Oxford features a young librarian named Avery. Avery is writing a fantasy novel and nursing a deep loss—his birth mother gave him up for adoption when he was a baby. Avery's character was inspired by our two sons, Jason and Jonathan, who were both adopted. Jason also writes fantasy, and Jonathan was adopted from the Mississippi Children's Home Society, as Avery was in this story. Part of the story is set during the annual Yoknapatawpha Summer Writers' Workshop, which Avery attends, and which I attended (in real life) for seven summers. It was fun to set scenes at all my favorite places in Oxford, including the library, the Depot, Square Books, and Uptown Coffee.

I think my favorite story in the collection is "Senatobia: John and Mary Margaret." It's about a biracial couple who dated at Ole Miss in the late 1960s, when this wasn't socially acceptable. At all. This is another story with quite a few scenes in Oxford, especially on the Ole Miss campus, where my husband and I were students just a few years after this story was set. Scenes at Mary Margaret's sorority house, the grove, and a football game were written from memories of my days on campus, but I did some research in order to write about the Black blues club John takes Mary Margaret to one night to hear Henry Cook and the Checkmates. All of this is just the "back story" for what happens fifty years later when John and Mary Margaret's lives intersect again, at the nursing home where both of their spouses now live, suffering from Alzheimer's and Lewy Body Disorder.

As "Adele" continues to travel the state speaking at libraries, she discovers ghosts and gypsies in Meridian, goes to a Miss Mississippi pageant in Vicksburg, meets a childhood friend of Jim Weatherly ("Midnight Train to Georgia") in Pontotoc, helps a victim of domestic abuse in Aberdeen, finds a kidnapped girl in West Point, bonds with a woman in Starkville who, like Adele, struggles with eating disorders due to childhood sexual abuse, and helps a young girl in Southaven who is being treated for cancer at St. Jude's Children's Hospital in Memphis.

I penned most of these stories in just a couple of months, early in 2018. The writing was fun and happened quickly. For many years I had heard writer friends say things like, "my characters take on a life of their own on the page," and I always rolled my eyes at them and said, or thought, "yeah, sure they do." Until I started writing these stories. With each story I started with the setting—the town I had visited—and fairly quickly chose a main character. Some of them were based very loosely on someone I had met at the library, but most of them just "came to me" and were pure products of an imagination that I didn't know I had! As William Faulkner said, "It begins with a character usually, and once he stands up on his feet and begins to move, all I can do is trot along behind him with a paper and pencil trying to keep up long enough to put down what he says and does." Yes! And what an exciting experience that was. Several people have asked me if I plan to write a "sequel" to *Friends of the Library*. There are so many more great little towns to visit—not only in Mississippi but all over the Southeast, especially—and I'm sure there are more stories to be told. As George Saunders said, "When you read a short story, you come out a little more aware and a little more in love with the world around you."

Six Books in Three Years: An Indie Publishing Journey
2019

The quickly changing world of book publishing can be a difficult terrain to traverse for a new writer. After spending a decade "prepping" for this leg of the journey by writing and publishing essays in various journals and magazines and building a platform on social media, I was finally ready to publish a book.

And then this happened: I published three in one year. And three more in the next two years. Here's the kicker: these six books are published by six different independent publishers, and I don't have a literary agent. I also don't have a "brand."

HOW IMPORTANT IS IT FOR AN AUTHOR TO HAVE A BRAND?

A lot has been written about the importance of having a "brand." This article in *HuffPost* says that a writer should maintain continuity in genre and voice. My readers tell me that I have a distinctive voice that reaches across genres, but my six books include four genres: memoir, novel, short story collection, and three essay anthologies (for which I was editor).

I get that it would be nice for readers to hear my name and think, "Oh, yes, Susan Cushman writes upmarket women's fiction, OR poignant memoir, OR confessional personal essays, OR character-driven southern short stories." Or even to be known as a consistent editor of anthologies, which is my most probable reputation at this point. But I didn't set out to do this—to write and publish in so many different genres. I think my journey is a reflection of my personality and life experiences. I love more than one kind of art and music, and I read in many genres.

Where to Start

In the beginning, I spent six years writing a novel before I queried over 100 literary agents for *Cherry Bomb* (Dogwood Press, August 2017). This process took over six months, as I carefully researched and found agents who represented "comparative titles," or so I thought. But twenty-four of the twenty-five agents who asked to read the full manuscript responded with similar praise for the prose but confusion about where to market the book. Is it southern literary fiction or narrative upmarket fiction? Could it work in the YA market? Finally, agent #100 fell in love with the book, or so she said. But after working with her and her editors for over a year, I parted ways with them. It became clear that we had different visions for the book, and I wasn't willing to turn it into commercial fiction like *Girl With the Dragon Tattoo*, which the agent suggested that I read in order to learn how to make my protagonist more "hard-ass." Nothing wrong with *Girl With the Dragon Tattoo*, by the way, but it wasn't the type of book I was writing.

Cherry Bomb has strong spiritual elements, is set in the south in the 1970s and 80s, and is full of art and religious imagery. So I walked away from hopes for a book deal with a large publisher and found a small press in Mississippi that shared my vision for the book.

Am I happy with my decision? Yes, in that this publisher preserved the integrity of the work. But I always recommend that new

writers try to query literary agents—the gatekeepers to the large houses—and then turn to indie presses if that doesn't work out. (I am still
considering querying agents for my next book.)

THE PROS AND CONS OF BEING AN INDIE WRITER

Since I was working without an agent, I was free to pursue different
publishers for my other books, which were unfolding at the same time as
the novel. When I found a small press for my memoir *Tangles and Plaques:
A Mother and Daughter Face Alzheimer's* (eLectio Publishing, January 2017),
they weren't aware that my novel was also coming out in 2017.

Neither was the university press who offered me a contract for my first
anthology, *A Second Blooming: Becoming the Women We Are Meant To Be*
(Mercer University Press, March 2017.). Of course it was exciting to
have three books published in 2017, but it was also a bit of a marketing
challenge. Fortunately many bookstores welcomed me for events for all
three books, and the crowds varied because of the different types of
books being offered.

DOING WHAT YOU LOVE

As those first three books were in various stages of pre-production,
publication, and marketing, I came to realize that what I was enjoying
the most was editing the anthology. So I decided to do another one. I
pitched *Southern Writers on Writing* (University Press of Mississippi, May
2018) to a fourth publisher, and they immediately offered me a contract. Working with twenty-six southern authors was an editor's dream.
The book was well-received, and my reputation as an editor was being
noticed.

One Project Leads to Another

In 2017 I went on a "library book tour" to speak at libraries in ten small towns in my home state of Mississippi. I was touring for my novel and my memoir, but I wasn't expecting what happened next. The towns themselves and the people who came to the library events inspired me to write a collection of linked short stories titled—what else?—*Friends of the Library*, which was published in August by Koehler Books.

Writing those stories was so much fun and so much easier than the novel. I'm visiting 24 libraries in seven southern states on my current book tour, so I'm considering a sequel: More *Friends of the Library*. But I haven't given up on writing another novel.

Back to What You Love

In the midst of finishing edits for *Friends of the Library*, I was contacted by Kathy L. Murphy, Founder of the Pulpwood Queens and Timber Guys Book Club Reading Nation, which has over 750 book clubs. I had been a participating author at the annual Pulpwood Queens Girlfriend Weekend several times, and she was planning a big celebration in 2020, which would mark the 20th anniversary of her organization. Kathy wanted an anthology with essays by authors and book club members to commemorate the anniversary, and she asked me to edit it. Of course I immediately said yes, and *The Pulpwood Queens Celebrate 20 Years!* released in December 2019 from a sixth independent publisher, Brother Mockingbird.

Mod Barbie, Elphaba, and the Yellow Rose of Texas
2019

My friend and fellow Tennessee author River Jordan called me up one day in 2009 to ask, "Hey, Susan, do you want to go on a road trip with me to Jefferson, Texas next January?" I thought, "What the heck is in Jefferson, Texas, and why would we want to go there?" River proceeded to describe in colorful detail the annual book convention hosted by Kathy L. Murphy for her 750+ book clubs, known as the Pulpwood Queens. The event was called Girlfriend Weekend.

"What do we do there?" I asked River.

"We dress up in crazy costumes. The authors speak on panels and visit with the book club members, then we all go and eat barbeque."

What's not to love about that? And to top it all off, my favorite author of all time, Pat Conroy, was going to be there! And Elizabeth Berg! This was pushing all my buttons.

There's an annual theme for the event, and for the January 2010 Girlfriend Weekend, there were two themes. On that Friday night we would be celebrating the 50th anniversary of Barbie and on Saturday night there would be a commemorative ball for the 70th anniversary of *The Wizard of Oz*. During the rest of the weekend, many of the authors and readers would dress in traditional Pulpwood Queens attire: tiaras (yes) and anything leopard print and hot pink.

So in January of 2010 I found myself tagging along with River to my first ever Girlfriend Weekend. I say "tagging along" because I really didn't fit into either of the categories to which the rest of the two hundred or more people belonged. I wasn't a published author yet (I had essays published in journals and magazines, but no book out) and I wasn't a member of one of the Pulpwood Queens Book Clubs. But I was an avid reader, and I was writing a book, so the weekend was truly a feast for my literary soul.

One of the highlights, of course, was meeting my literary idol, Pat Conroy. *The Prince of Tides* is my all-time favorite book (and movie). When I saw Pat wearing an apron and serving barbeque to a room full of book club members, I loved him even more. But when I saw him standing in line to get several new authors to sign their books for him—books he purchased—I was speechless. All the authors were like this—there weren't dividing lines between the *New York Times* best-selling authors and the first-time authors and the readers. Everyone joined together to celebrate books. To celebrate stories.

On Friday night when I saw Nicole Seitz dressed as "Cicada Barbie" with giant insect wings, in honor of her newly published novel *Saving Cicadas*, I had to have my picture taken with her. (I was "Mod Barbie.") We bonded over conversations about writing and our shared Christian faith, and ever since, Nicole has been a mentor to me, encouraging and guiding me through the publication of six books. Our relationship is symbiotic, as Nicole contributed essays to two of my anthologies, and she crafted the original artwork for the cover for the Pulpwood Queens anthology.

Since Saturday evening was the Great Big Ball of Hair Ball, with *The Wizard of Oz* as its theme, I went as the Wicked Witch, wearing a black hat and wig, and a green T-shirt that read, "The Flying Monkeys scarred me for life." This was before the musical *Wicked*, but I already had a love for Elphaba, and similar wounds from childhood. The weekend was fun, but it left me wanting more. I wanted to come back as a Pulpwood Queens author. It took eight years for that dream to come true.

In January of 2018 I returned to Girlfriend Weekend, dressing as an artsy hippie for the "Bohemian Rhapsody" theme. Two of my books were official Pulpwood Queens Book Club selections: *A Second Blooming: Becoming the Women We Are Meant to Be* was the February selection that year. It is an anthology I edited with essays by twenty women, several of whom were already Pulpwood Queen authors. My novel *Cherry Bomb* was a bonus book for March. It was surreal being on two panels that weekend, and later Skyping with several book clubs, some as far away as Las Vegas, Nevada! Another highlight of the 2018 weekend for me was the keynote speech by author Lisa Wingate, who wrote my favorite book of the year, *Before We Were Yours*.

And what a joy to return in 2019 for the "How the West Was Won" weekend. My second anthology, *Southern Writers on Writing*, was the January official book selection, and our panel of contributing authors kicked off the weekend's celebration. I loved meeting Paula McLain and hearing her keynote. I had read and loved all of her novels, and when I got home, I read her memoir, *Like Family: Growing Up in Other People's Houses*, about her experiences as a foster child, which endeared her to me even more. It was equally fun to reunite with fellow authors I don't see in person frequently and to visit with book club members from all over the country. Although the Pulpwood Queens are an international group and not primarily southern, I loved being with fellow Mississippi authors such as Michael Farris Smith, Johnnie Bernhard, and Julie Cantrell, who isn't really from Mississippi but had lived in Oxford quite a few years. And my fellow Tennessee authors, River Jordan (who also gave a great keynote) and newcomer and fellow Memphian, Claire Fullerton, who was on a panel for her excellent novel *Mourning Dove*.

There is a large Pulpwood Queens Book Club in my hometown of Jackson, Mississippi, and they always show up in spades. Groups from many other states came to the 2019 event, and a great time was had by all, especially at the ball on Saturday night. Line dancing in costumes as hilarious as cows with protruding udders, a woman dressed as an oil well, and quite a few courageous women who represented the music, literature, and history of the west. I went as the Yellow Rose of Texas. We celebrated our love for each other and our shared love for books at the best literary event in the country.

Writing *John and Mary Margaret*: Crossing the Color Divide
(March 2022)

In the spring and summer of 2020, two cataclysmic crises were happening all over America. Covid was on the rise with no vaccines in sight. And many Americans were rising up against a myriad of brutal acts of racial injustice. It was a perfect storm. Sitting in my office at home in Memphis, Tennessee, I wanted to join the protests out on the streets, but Covid and my age (I was 69 at the time) made that a dangerous proposition. I aired my frustration to my husband, wanting my voice to be heard. "You are a writer," he said. "What better situation for a writer than to be isolated at home?" As Eudora Welty once said, "Every writer, like everybody else, thinks he's living through the crisis of the ages. To write honestly and with all our powers is the least we can do, and the most."

I was born in Jackson, Mississippi, in 1951 and came of age in the 1960s Jim Crow South. When I graduated from high school in 1969, there were fewer than a dozen Black students in our school of over 1,200. The following year busing to achieve integration would change the landscape of our historically segregated education system in Jackson and other parts of the South forever. But I left to attend the University of Mississippi that fall, moving from one privileged White bubble to another. Little did I know that fifty years later I would write a book about a Black boy from Memphis and a White girl from Jackson who fall in love on the Ole Miss campus in 1966.

John and Mary Margaret spans over fifty years of civil rights history, mostly in Mississippi and Memphis. A big part of my impetus to write this novel came from my love for my four mixed-race granddaughters: two of them with their wonderful African American father (my son-in-law) and beautiful South Korean mother (my daughter;) and two more with my precious South Korean son and his loving Hmong wife. In addition to my love for my family, I was having a growing "awakening" to so much civil rights history that I never learned growing up and wasn't aware of as an adult.

My "awakening" that spring and summer was fed greatly by reading Isabel Willkerson's amazing book, *Caste*, along with numerous newspaper articles and books by other Black authors. As I sat down to write this book, I immediately realized that I needed "sensitivity readers"—Black readers who could help me walk through the mine-field of a White woman writing about a Black male protagonist. Telling John's story would be a challenge. From his childhood and teenage years in Memphis through several decades of his life, I would l need help portraying his culture, and especially his words and the way he used them.

John Abbott's character was inspired by Don Cole and Kenneth Mayfield—real-life members of the "Ole Miss Eight"—and two of sixty Black students who were arrested during a protest on campus in 1970. Doing the research to set his story as accurately as possible in the middle of historic events was the easy part. Getting his character right took help from two wonderful Black authors, Jeffrey Blount and Ralph Eubanks.

While it's true that writing Margaret Sutherland's story was easier—a White girl from Jackson, like me, attending Ole Miss in the 1960s—I still asked several women who were in my sorority (Delta Delta Delta) to read an early draft and give me feedback, especially since several scenes were set in our sorority house. My memory for details fifty years later isn't always sharp, so I really appreciated their help!

As I went on a book tour in June of 2021, I was blessed to

receive positive feedback from a Black male book club in Memphis, as well as diverse groups of southerners at events in Tennessee, South Carolina, Florida, Alabama, and Mississippi. My courage was helped by these words from James Campbell, author of *Talking at the Gates: A Life of James Baldwin*, and other works. Writing in the *Wall Street Journal* in January of 2021, Campbell said: "Writers on each side of the color line have more than just the right to cross the divide and report back. It is their duty. Imaginative life depends on cultural exchange. Literature depends on the imagination. To put it another way, culture *is* cultural appropriation. Any artist worth the name should be willing to take a punch for it."

III

Alzheimer's, Caregiving, Death, and Dying

Early on the afternoon of July 9, Dad awoke briefly from his coma-like sleep, smiled and made eye contact with Mom and me for the first time in twenty-four hours. He responded to our words by squeezing our hands. And then he was gone—the most powerful sunset I've ever seen.

—Susan Cushman, *"Watching"*

I've always been a person to whom "forgive and forget" has seemed absurdly unworkable…. Since witnessing my grandmother's Alzheimer's, I've begun to wonder whether a small reversal wouldn't better suit humanity. Maybe it would be more practical if forgetting proceeded forgiving. Maybe happiness would be more easily achieved if we all made a practice of forgetting.

—Robert Leleux, *The Living End: A Memoir of Forgetting and Forgiving*

The Glasses
2010

"I can't get my glasses clean." Mom was riding with me to do some shopping when she pulled her glasses off and held them up to the windshield for a better view of the smudges.

"Here. I've got a special cloth for cleaning lenses," I offered.

She fumbled with the cloth for a few minutes. At a stoplight, I took the glasses and tried to clean them for her.

"Mom, these are all scratched up . . . in fact, these are your old glasses. Where are the new ones we got you?"

"Oh, I think they fell under my bed."

"Well, when we get back to your apartment, I'll look for them."

"Oh, no. You couldn't possibly fit under the bed. There's only a tiny, tiny space there."

"But I could at least see if they're there, and maybe fish them out with a yardstick or something."

"No, there just isn't room under that bed, I promise you."

"Well, I'll still look for them when we get back."

After shopping we went to lunch. Trying to read the menu, Mom took her glasses off and said, "These glasses are so dirty, I can't see a thing through them."

"That's because they're scratched, Mom, remember? I'm going to look for your new glasses when we get back to your apartment."

"Oh, don't worry about it. I'm sure they'll turn up some time."

After lunch, I took her to get a manicure and pedicure. Sitting across from her and reading fashion magazines while a cute guy did her nails, I realized we'd been together for three hours, and I hadn't asked her any of the questions I'd been thinking about from my childhood. They'd have to wait 'til we got back to her place now. Or I could just listen as she entertained the employees and other customers at the nail place.

"This is my little girl." She pointed to me. "She lives in Memphis. She took my car away and sold my house. But she comes to visit me about once a year."

I smile at the young women in the chairs next to her, fighting back the urge to defend myself. One of them gives me a knowing wink, which helps. And then the young man doing Mom's nails says, "Now, Mrs. Johnson, your daughter brought you in here just a month ago to get your nails done, didn't she?"

"Oh, I don't know. She lives in Memphis. Ouch!"

"Sorry. I didn't realize your toe was tender."

"Well, it is. Something's wrong with it. I've been meaning to get someone to look at it."

The nail on the big toe of her right foot was thick and green with fungus.

"Mom, I took you to the doctor last month and she told us what to do about it. Remember? I got you some Vicks VapoRub to put on it twice a day. I wrote you a note and taped it to the Vicks bottle by your bed. Have you been putting it on your toe?"

The giggles the other customers had been trying to stifle just couldn't be held in any longer at this. So I said to the room, "I know it sounds ridiculous, but Mom's internist told us that more than one of her patients have had success with this."

A few minutes later, as we're leaving the nail place, with Mom wearing a pair of free, disposable flip-flops, she looks at her feet and says, "What's wrong with the nail on that big toe?"

"You've got a fungus, Mom."

"Oh. Is there anything we can do about it?"

"We can try putting Vicks VapoRub on it. I've got some for you back at your apartment."

"Vicks? Really? Well, I'll try anything once!"

Back in the car, we're driving through a neighborhood that had been hit by tornadoes a couple of weeks ago. Mom says, "I think I saw this on the news, but I didn't realize how bad it was."

"Me, either. Wow—look at that huge tree completely uprooted over there. And all those houses with blue tarps on the roofs where trees fell on them. My goodness."

At this Mother took off her glasses and held them up to the window. "I can't really see them well. My glasses are so dirty. Do you have something I can clean them with?"

"We already cleaned them, Mom. They're scratched. Those are your old glasses. We need to find your new ones when we get back to your apartment."

"What new ones?"

"The ones you think might have fallen under your bed."

"Oh, don't worry about it, these are fine."

Back at Ridgeland Pointe, Mom's assisted living facility, we make our way through the lobby, where she "introduces" me to all her friends. Again. Finally we're back in her apartment and I'm on my hands and knees looking under her bed for the glasses.

"You can't see anything under there, Susan. The space is just too small."

"I can see fine, Mom, but there's nothing under here."

Up off my knees, I begin to search her bedside table, and finally the bookcase headboard behind her pillow.

"Here they are, Mom!"

I hand her the glasses, and she looks at them, then at me, and says, "Oh. I like my old ones better. But thanks, anyway."

An Unexpected Gift
2017

Yesterday was my bi-monthly visit with my mother at Lakeland Nursing Home. If you're new to my blog, Mom is 81 and has Alzheimer's.

As I drove down to visit her, I received a phone call from a dear friend in Memphis. Her mother had fallen and was in the hospital. Another friend's mother had also fallen, a few days ago, and is now staying with her daughter and family as they decide if she can return to her home, assisted living, or other options. And yet a third friend emailed me with news of her father's recent diagnosis with cancer. This business of getting old is complicated, I think, by two things in particular, and probably a whole slew of things in general. The specific things I'm thinking of now are:

1. People are living longer, due to medical advances, and

2. Families don't stay together as much as they once did. Many other cultures continue to have extended families living under one roof, while we Americans want "our space" and to live our lives unhindered by the burden of around-the-clock care of aging parents. (I do have several friends who have their elderly parents living with them. They are better people than I could ever be.)

Anyway, when I visited with Mom on Monday, she did recognize me. "This is my little girl!" she told the ladies in the wheelchairs on either side of her in the hall.

"Oh, she looks just like you!" one of them said, and I thanked her. I think my mother is beautiful.

After our usual interaction about practical matters, which are completely lost on her now (I washed and ironed two of your blouses,

Mom, and I'm putting them in your closet now. Where is my closet? It's right across from your bed.) I wheeled Mom up to the front lobby where we could visit and share a piece of coffee cake from Starbucks.

I entered her world, as I always do, and complimented her, again, for her landscaping work on the patio (which of course she had nothing to do with) and showed her (again) photographs of her great-granddaughter, Grace, whom she can't fathom, as she struggles to remember even her grandchildren at this point. She can no longer form complete sentences, but speaks in fragments, sometimes apologizing that she can't remember a word, a person, a place.

But suddenly, she smiled at me and said, "I love your hair!"

"Really? I haven't had it this short in years. I'm glad you like it."

"It's very flattering."

Smile. "Thank you, Mom. I really like yours long, in a ponytail, like you wore it when you were young."

This conversation was repeated three to four times, which didn't bother me at all. I could have listened to her praise and compliments all day. They were rare for most of my life. And even though she was talking about something as mundane as a haircut, coming from someone who, when she was "in her right mind," usually criticized me for being fat, having bad hair, etc., this was like healing oil being poured on a wound. At age 58, I was finally receiving praise and approval from my mother.

If this sounds silly to you, you might as well just quit reading this blog post now. Just move along. There's nothing to see here. But if this strikes a chord with you, please keep reading, because it gets better.

As I was about to leave, the sky was getting dark and it began to rain.

"Mom, it's going to be thunder storming, and I need to drive back to Memphis, so I'd better leave soon."

Mom's smile faded, and she reached out, grabbed my hand, held it tightly, closed her eyes and *prayed*:

"Oh, Lord, we ask you to protect Susan as she drives. Take care of her and keep her safe…." She went on and on, for several sentences, speaking with complete clarity.

Tears ran down my face as I listened to my mother, who usually can't speak a full sentence, pray with such beauty and ease. I don't remember my mother ever praying for me, with me, like that. Ever. All the years of verbal and emotional abuse that I suffered from her seemed to melt. Forgiveness gushed from my soul as I listened to her prayer.

When she finished, she opened her eyes, smiled, and kissed me on the lips.

I drove home to Memphis through the rain with no difficulties, and with an unusual peace. When I told my husband the story at home tonight, I said, "her prayer reminded me of my father, who was an excellent Bible teacher and prayed beautifully."

"She was replaying the tape of your father's prayers," my husband offered. And I wept at his words, picturing my parents, doing their daily devotionals together every morning. Dad was eloquent. As an elder in their Presbyterian church, he preached many sermons during interims when they didn't have a pastor. And he led evangelism seminars and taught Sunday School classes. And of course I thought that some day when my mind is struggling to hold on, that my own dear husband's prayers will be my salvation.

For all the dysfunction of my family of origin, today I am thankful for this unexpected gift of prayer from my mother's lips. Alzheimer's might be taking her mind, but God still has her heart, as broken and wounded as it is. I pray that He will protect her soul in the coming months and years that she might have left on this earth, and sustain the peace and forgiveness that I experienced today, by His grace.

End-of-Life Issues
2017

Until a few weeks ago, Mom seemed content in her ever-shrinking world—paddling around in her wheelchair at Lakeland Nursing Home, smiling at everyone. And then she had another fall, which escalated to dehydration, a urinary tract infection and ecoli, and eventually pneumonia. So she's been in the hospital for one week today.

The first five days in the hospital, Mom was pretty incoherent. Didn't open her eyes much and was unresponsive to verbal commands and questions. But on Wednesday that changed. Maybe the IV fluids finally helped her wake up, and she began to respond verbally. Up until then, I was thinking this was going to be her swan song. She made it clear that she doesn't want any "extreme measures" and has a DNR order. So, even something as mildly invasive as a peg (stomach feeding tube) seemed extreme to me.

But with her returned alertness, I was advised by five professionals (three physicians and two priests)—two of whom are related to her—that a peg would be a compassionate measure, not an extreme one. The peg tube would hopefully allow her to get enough nutrition that she could get off the IVs and return to the nursing home, where she could be mobile again. One friend, who is an RN, agreed, saying that long-term IVs can be painful. But another doctor told me he doesn't think she will ever eat orally again, which makes the peg seem a bit more like an extreme measure. Like so many important issues in life—and especially end-of-life issues—nothing here is black and white. So I signed the papers for the peg tube. As I write these words, Mom is having the procedure done.

I've been here before—first with my father, in 1998. And then with my aunt. Next it was my brother, Mike Johnson, who died six years ago this month. And finally Urania, my dear friend in Memphis who also died in 2007. But each of these folks were in the final stages of cancer when we were facing those end-of-life issues. It was clear that they were dying, and *why* they were dying. With Mom, it's not so clear. Without the peg, it's possible she would starve to death, which doesn't seem humane. But even with the peg, she could be bedridden for weeks, months or even years, which also doesn't seem humane. When nothing else causes death, the Alzheimer's patient's system eventually just shuts down because her brain forgets how to run it. I pray for Mother's comfort, and for wisdom in making decisions that are compassionate.

As I walk the halls of Baptist Hospital, I'm struck by the acrylic signs strategically placed on the walls. Each one contains a scripture verse. The one across from me in the waiting room right now says this: "Those who trust in the Lord for help will find their strength renewed."—Isaiah 40:31

I imagine those words are helpful to friends and family who are visiting loved ones in the hospital. But I don't know if Mom can trust in the Lord in her diminished mental state. Sometimes when I visit her in the nursing home I sing old hymns, and she sings along on some of them. Other times I've recited the 23rd Psalm, and she joins me. So I know that these lifelong elements of her Presbyterian faith are etched on her psyche. Or somewhere. But now when I hold her hand and say a prayer, she just looks at me, through glazed-over eyes. I wonder what she hears. And I hope that God hears.

Mom doesn't know who anyone is any more. Not even me—although she smiles when she sees me. And once, yesterday, she said, "I love you, too," after I told her I loved her. Usually she just says, "thank you." I brought a picture of Dad and her up to the hospital from her room at the nursing home and put it in her hands yesterday. She ran her fingers over the picture and said, "That looks like something important." Indeed. They were married for 49 years before cancer took my father at the young age of 68. He was the love of her life, so yes, Mom, this is definitely something important. And today I find myself asking, "What would my father—her spouse of 49 years—do?" It's too late to ask him whether or not to do the peg, since it's already happening. But other hard decisions may be coming, so tomorrow I think I'll drive out to his grave and sit on the nearby bench under that beautiful tree and have a chat with him. My brother is buried a few feet away. And my precious Goddaughter's grave is also another nearby. I always feel like I'm surrounded by a great cloud of witnesses when I'm sitting on that bench. Each of them is a hero in one way or another. And I could sure use a hero right about now.

Watching
2011

"I hope it's soon." Her voice is calm, with a touch of weariness.

"An theli o Theos," I stumble on the Greek phrase, which means "God willing." She nods and smiles at my effort.

We're sitting in a tiny study that opens onto the balcony at my friend's retirement home in Germantown, a suburb of Memphis. It's a corner apartment, facing southwest. An hour ago the view from the balcony was cinematic. The sun's late afternoon rays had been diffused by a gathering of milky clouds, slightly backlit, leaving an artist's dream sky in its setting wake. Just when I thought it was gone, it made a brief encore appearance at the horizon—more intense than its hazy afternoon showing. Now I look at my friend and wonder if her departure will follow this pattern.

Urania is eighty six. She has end stage metastatic bone cancer. I'm spending a few days with her between her children's shifts, which have increased in frequency and duration over the past few weeks. Her daughters live in New York City, and my mother lives in Mississippi, so Urania and I sort of adopted each other a few years back. I'm not the only one who considers her their unofficial "yia yia." She takes everyone in, regardless of race, religion, or socio-economic status. Years ago, when she and her husband owned a Canada Dry Bottling Company, one of the teenage boys they "took in" to work at the plant was Elvis Presley. They thought he needed a break.

She took *us* in—the women and daughters at Saint John Orthodox Church. Most of us are converts to her Greek Orthodox faith. She opened her home for monthly gatherings, where we learned more about our adopted faith. She hosted a monthly book club, right up until two weeks before her death. She taught us how to make lamb soup for Easter and kolliva (boiled wheat) for memorial services. She oversaw the decoration of the funeral bier with fresh flowers and greenery for Holy Friday.

"Father Troy came and heard my confession and served me communion last week." Her speech is slow and her breathing is labored. "My grandchildren and friends have all visited. I've said my goodbyes."

She closes the book she's been reading, *The Kite Runner*, before asking me to bring her a Vanilla Slim Fast with a straw from the refrigerator. "It's my dessert," she says. An hour or two earlier, she had eaten a small portion of shrimp and pasta which her son, George, had prepared while he was here this weekend.

Everyday actions take on a larger significance when someone is near death. Will *The Kite Runner* be the last book she ever reads? Will her last earthly sustenance be something as mundane as a can of Slim Fast?

When I help her into bed later and kiss her goodnight, all my senses are tuned to the life force in her room, which seems mystically charged, as if the angels are holding their breath.

She squeezes my hand and says, "I love you."

"I love you, too."

"Forgive me, Susan... I'm too weak to kneel or even stand in front of my icons to pray tonight." She adjusts the oxygen tubes as I pull the covers up over her frail body. "I'll have to pray in bed." Her voice fades, her eyes close, and her lips move silently for a minute, and then she's still. The prayer is working. And the Darvocet.

Turning to leave her room, I cross myself and kiss the large icon of the Mother of God on the wall near her bed and whisper, "Lord, let thy servant depart in peace." And then, silently, *oh, please, God, grant her a painless death.* Tears fill my eyes. Picking up the little red *Pocket Prayer*

Book for Orthodox Christians from the small table underneath her icons, I find "A Prayer for the Sick." And then I say the Jesus Prayer–the ancient mantra she's taught me: "Kirie, Jesus Christe, eleison me, ton amartalon." *Lord Jesus Christ, Son of God, have mercy on me a sinner.* I've seen her go to a place inside herself with these words… sometimes before having a medical procedure, and especially during her husband's long illness and death five years ago. They had been married fifty-nine years.

The nightlight casts a glimmer on the gold leaf of the halos on the icons. The oxygen pump makes a steady *whoosh…whoosh.* I lean over her bed in the semi-darkness, listening for the sound of her breathing. There it is, matching the rhythm of the machine breath for breath. I want to stay and watch with her through the night, but I need to sleep, to keep up my strength for the days ahead. Reluctantly I drag myself away from her presence.

Pouring myself a glass of wine and getting the coffee pot ready to turn on in the morning, I take a deep breath. This feels so familiar, this *watching.* I've been here before.

The first time was in 1998. Dad had been a marathon runner for over fifteen years. Boston. New York. All the big ones. He even completed a triathlon when he was in his 60s. Affectionately called "the Guru of Running" by the members of the Mississippi Track Club, he and my mother owned Bill Johnson's Phidippides Sports in Jackson from 1982-1997. They closed the business in May of 1997, just two weeks before Dad's surgery to remove one of his lungs. Fourteen months later, Dad lost his battle with cancer, at the age of sixty-eight.

I moved in to help Mom a week before he died. What the three of us shared during that final week of my father's life was the best and worst that we can know in this life. We labored through the days and suffered through the nights, touching heaven and earth simultaneously.

The intimacy I craved with my parents while growing up—that elusive soul connection—came late to the party and with abandon.

I watched my parents' marriage of 49 years turn on its head under the stress of my father's impending death. With all the distractions removed–business, church, running, travel, social opportunities–they were left face to face with their brokenness. Fortunately, they had soft hearts and a strong faith. I watched as their frustration and anger leaked out. Then I watched with admiration at the reconciliation and forgiveness that followed those moments of raw truth and emotion.

Mom and I were Dad's tag team. Just as she ran out of physical and emotional energy, I stepped in, and the pace stepped up. As his anxiety level increased, higher doses of morphine were prescribed. Forty-eight hours before his death, his suffering reached its apex and he asked for more meds. I told him that if I gave him more, he would no longer be able to communicate with us. He knew it was time. I witnessed my parents' last conversation before Dad began the final leg of his journey.

Sometimes it's hard for family members to let go, especially where food is involved. Mom had been cooking for my father for forty-nine years, so when he wanted less and less food in the final days and hours of his life, she had to turn the feeding and medication over to me. It was just too painful for her. Grinding up morphine tablets into applesauce for breakfast. Crushed ice for lunch. More morphine, this time in a tablespoon of banana pudding for supper. The Hospice nurse had explained it to Mom and me—how our loved one was being fed heavenly food as he pulled away from his earthly life. He can leave more peacefully if his family embraces the process and doesn't hold on too tightly.

They had told us about how the person dying sometimes experiences a final surge of alertness and energy, just before the end. I watched for this, even as Dad slept through most of his final morning on the hospital bed in my parents' living room. And then it happened. Just like the sunset off Urania's balcony in Memphis nine years later. Early on the afternoon of July 9, Dad awoke briefly from his coma-like sleep, smiled and made eye contact with Mom and me for the first time in twenty-four hours. He responded to our words by squeezing our hands. And then he was gone—the most powerful sunset I've ever seen.

As we stood there holding his hands, I was struck by the complexity of our grief, which was infused with a peace that came from knowing we had done what we could. All that Jesus had asked of His disciples at Gethsemane, as He faced His death, was that they *watch* with Him. We had been *watching*.

I awake at 7 am on Tuesday to the sounds of silence in the guest room at Urania's apartment, and hurry to check on her status, stopping only briefly in the kitchen to turn on the coffee pot. *Whoosh… whoosh…* the oxygen pump greets me. My heart skips a beat as I stop to watch for signs of life. Her tiny body rises and falls with her shallow breathing. She's still here. I exhale quietly.

Facing the icon of Christ in her prayer corner, I pray: "Lord, grant me to greet the coming day in peace." *Kiss.* And again before the large icon of the Holy Virgin: "It is truly meet to bless thee, O Theotokos, who art ever blessed and most pure and the Mother of our God." *Kiss.* Quietly I slip out of her room.

Two cups of coffee later I hear her calling. She's awake and ready to dress and have breakfast. She's weaker today, and I suggest it might be time to call Hospice. Urania agrees and we call her son who lives in town. An evaluation will be arranged. She discusses this as though scheduling an oil change for her car. After the nurse leaves she naps for an hour or two. The ratio of sleeping to waking hours continues to shift as her body begins to pull away from this world.

During the afternoon, amidst a flurry of phone calls from Urania's sons, daughters, and daughters-in-law, she clings a little more tenaciously to her independence, putting up a strong front. It isn't denial. It's a mother's irrational but unselfish last attempt at protecting her children from the pain of loss. Oh, she knows they are losing her, but she doesn't want to inconvenience them, to disrupt the busy, meaningful and productive lives they have carved out for themselves. Urania is a second generation Greek immigrant, and her strength and beauty have given them what they need to become the successful people they are today. It's been her joy to watch them live out their adult years with such fullness. But the love she gave them is the same love that is now calling them home, to her death bed. Careers and other commitments would be worked around. It's their turn to watch.

In the interim, each day that is given to me to be with Urania, each moment, is a gift. Like tonight, when my husband, the Associate Pastor at our church, comes to visit. He opens *The Book of Needs* to pray with her.

Urania asks if she can read something first. Her favorite Scripture, Psalm 104. *All thirty-five verses.* Each word is a struggle. I offer to read it for her, but she shakes her head, *no.* Her voice trembles, then breaks. We are privy to her uncharacteristic tears when she gets to verse 33:

> *I will sing to the Lord as long as I live; I will sing praise to my*
> *God while I have my being.*

Her being overshadows our weak efforts at comforting her. She comforts us. We are only watching.

Wednesday morning, October 3, at Urania's apartment, she's still asleep at 8 a.m. At breakfast she eats only a few bites and has difficulty trying to swallow the three large pills she takes from the daily dose container she always keeps by her placemat.

"What are those, anyway?" I ask.

"Calcium and vitamins."

We look at each other, our thoughts converging. How important are calcium and vitamins to someone whose blood can no longer produce platelets? She puts the pills in a napkin, folds it up, and hands it to me for disposal in the kitchen trash. I'm watching… as she takes another step away from this temporal home.

At ten our pastor arrives. We chat about my upcoming trip to Greece. He shares stories of his visit there a few years ago. The book, *The Summer of My Greek Taverna*— one of the books I read in preparation for my trip and then loaned to Urania—is open on her ottoman, having displaced *The Kite Runner* as the current "last book Urania was reading" entry. While reading it during the three days I've been with her, she has giggled from time to time and I've asked what's so funny. "There are some things you have to be Greek to understand." Her family is from Cephalonia, the beautiful island featured in the movie, "Captain Corelli's Mandolin."

We're supposed to leave on our trip in nine days, but I'd rather be with her as she is dying than be in Greece, in the country of her ancestors. And it will break my heart to miss her funeral. But the trip was planned months ago, and involves another couple, airline, hotel, and ferry boat reservations. And, as the Greeks themselves say, "What can you do?" Urania says to me, "Light a candle for me at the church on Patmos. It's better to have you with me now than after I'm gone."

Father Troy serves her Communion. Each time could be the last, but then she will see God face to face and will no longer need the shadow. Watching her spirituality being tested as death crouches at her door, I know that I am in the presence of one who *loves* God. Not just one who *believes*.

Holy Communion strengthens her soul even as her body weakens. Her afternoon nap is longer than yesterday's. And then, it's time for me to leave. My three-day window is over. Her son, Tene, will be with her tonight, and others are coming into town the following day. I sit silently with her for a few minutes, watching her struggle to find the breath to express her feelings. Maybe words aren't necessary at this point. Touch would be better. So I kneel on the floor in front of her chair and we embrace. And then we share a parting kiss. On the lips. Her breath is infused with the rarified air of the spiritual world. "I'll call you tomorrow," I say, as I leave her apartment.

I make it down the hall before the pain erupts in my chest. *Aaaarrrrrgggghhhhh!* I scream and kick the walls of the elevator that is taking me away from her. As I drive home, my cell phone rings. It's Julia, one of her daughters, calling from New York. I pull myself back together and tell her about her mother's day. Probably the last day I will spend with her.

The next morning, my call is answered by Miss Betty, the private duty nurse. "She's much weaker this morning. Wants to stay in her nightgown today."

I ask to speak with her.

"I had a rough night," she begins. "I had to get up several times. It's good that Tene (her son) was here, because I'm pretty much dead weight now." Her words, not mine.

"You're lighter than air, Urania, but yes, it's good that Tene is with you. It's his place to give back some of the life you gave him, you know?"

She doesn't answer. I'm aching to be with her, but not wanting to take up space that isn't mine. I can see her sweet smile and the twinkle in her eyes, both fading as she continues to pull away from the shadow land. I can imagine the brilliance of her transfigured countenance, bathed in celestial light.

Being with her during these days has felt like a visit to a sacred place. Whenever I return from a trip to the monastery I frequent in Michigan, it's almost painful to re-enter everyday life. The business of getting meals, doing laundry, and paying bills feels like an intrusion. That's how it feels today. Except that I think I've brought some of her goodness home with me. My steps feel a bit lighter, and my mind flows to happy memories of times spent with Urania over the fifteen or more years I've known her.

It's afternoon again, and my thoughts return to her as sunset approaches, so I give her another call. This time she answers the phone and her voice is a little stronger. Wanting to hallow this conversation, I choose my final words carefully. "May God grant you a peaceful sleep."

"I love you, Susan."

"I love you, too."

I can hardly breathe when I hang up the phone at my house in Memphis and try to shift gears. To prepare for my weekend plans… the plans Urania was insistent that I keep. I'm going on a weekend fishing trip with my friend, Daphne, and her four kids. They live in Little Rock. We'll be meeting at Mountain View, Arkansas, on the White River, where she's reserved a cabin at Jack's Fishing Resort. "Resort" is a bit of a stretch for the facilities there, but the river is beautiful and the trees just glow in the fall. We've been there before. But this time, I'll think of Urania at sunset. And I'll still be *watching*.

I call Urania's house at 10 am on Friday, before leaving for Arkansas. Miss Betty, the sitter, answers the phone.

"How is she?" I ask.

"Not good," Betty's voice is quiet.

"Is she up?"

"No. And she hasn't eaten anything since yesterday. She barely spoke to Tene this morning. The Hospice nurse will be here soon."

"Good. They'll be a great help now. Please tell her I called and I love her."

Click. I ache to be with her, but I keep packing.

Driving from Memphis to Mountain View, Arkansas. I stop in Locust Grove and call Father Troy on my cell, thinking I might lose the signal as I ascend down the valley into Mountain View. The sun is bright, just before it slips behind the foothills. The clouds are dark and threatening. The contrast is vivid. Autumn is late this year—everything is still green with a few tinges of brown and orange.

"Did you see Urania today?" I ask, as my phone cackles with a bit of static. I'm at the edge of the Ozark National Forest.

"Yes. I spent about three hours with her."

A pang of envy strikes my heart. "How was she?"

"She slept a lot. But I read the Canon with her, and cried. Then the Hospice nurse gave her some Morphine, and I helped turn her and make her more comfortable once or twice. Mainly I sat with her." It's his turn to watch.

I weep as I picture my priest's tears of love and sadness mingling with his prayers for this woman who has been so important to him… to all of us whose lives she's touched. And changed.

A half hour later I'm driving into Mountain View. The first thing I see is a cemetery. I cross myself. Just down the road I stop at the main intersection. If you turn right, you end up at Wal Mart. But that's true at most intersections in Arkansas. There's a man sitting in the back of a pickup truck in front of me. He has a ponytail with streaks of grey and a striking profile—a chiseled Roman nose, high cheek bones, and a sunken amber jaw. The sign behind him says, "Live music on the square tonight."

Turning off Highway 5 at 5:45 pm into Jack's Fish Resort, I hurry to check in and get to the deck behind Jo Jo's Catfish Wharf for sunset on the White River. It's pretty, but it can't compete with the view from Urania's balcony earlier in the week. So I soothe myself with the best hushpuppies in the world, mediocre catfish, and melt-in-your-mouth chocolate cream pie. But they're just shadows.

Daphne and her kids arrive at 8:30 and we settle into our rental house for the night. It backs up to the river. The plan is to rise early to go fishing. I'm asleep as soon as my head hits the pillow.

Father Troy calls at 6:30 am. Saturday morning. When I hear my cell phone ringing, I know.

"She died at 5:30 this morning. George [her son] was with her… and Mary [his wife]."

"Today is my husband's birthday." My first words in response have nothing to do with Urania's death, but are a way of marking the day… a kind of double significance. I'll call him later at his hotel in Chicago, where's he's at a meeting. But now I open again the red *Prayer Book*, this time to page 24: "A Prayer For the Dead":

> *Into Thy hands, O Lord, I commend the soul of Thy servant, Urania… grant her rest, where all thy blessed saints repose, and where the light of Thy countenance shineth forth….*

At 7:30 am I'm lured to the kitchen by the enticing aroma of bacon frying. Daphne sees the news on my face and I cry into her arms. We tell her four children about my friend, Urania. They know about loss—they just lost their aunt Debbie four weeks ago. Daphne's sister

was only fifty one. Her family's grief mingles with mine today, temper-
ing our activities with a gentle overlay of somberness. The joy I share
with her and her children as we spend the day fishing on the White River and later experiencing a bit of the local music scene on the square
in downtown Mountain View is made fuller by reminders of Urania's
spirit of beauty and celebration. She's probably watching *me* now.

On Sunday morning I drive home from Mountain View and
go straight to St. John and upstairs to the nave, where Urania's body
was brought on Saturday. The casket is on the solea, in front of the
icon of Christ. Her presence in the church brings on another round of
weeping. And yes, I'm happy that she didn't suffer greatly and that she's
with her beloved Andy. He left this world five years ago. Of course I'm
thankful that she is with God now. But the hole she leaves in my heart,
in our church, our community, is significant.

I find each of her children before the service, during Visitation,
and we share stories and hugs. Her younger daughter, Theresa, is smiling, calmly comforting the visitors as they arrive. But then I see Julia,
and I fall completely apart in her arms. Julia is Urania's oldest daughter.
She moved her membership to St. John in Memphis when St. Nicholas
Greek Orthodox Church, her parish in New York City, was demolished
underneath the collapse of the World Trade Centers in 2001.

How many times will my grief leak out so physically? I'm still
in Julia's arms, shaking and crying noisily when a hush falls over the
church. I turn around to see that everyone else is already seated. It's
time for the Trisagion Prayers for the Dead. So I leave Julia to sit on
the front pew with her family, and I find my way to the back, and to my
friends. We comfort each other as we join in the prayers and hymns.

Again I'm overcome with tears, especially as we sing, "Memory Eternal," and when Father Troy gives a brief talk about Urania.
And then the vigil begins. I join one of my Goddaughters, Sarah, at

the reader's stand and we begin reading the Psalms, interspersed with a Prayer for the Departed. People sign up for one-hour "slots" to read during the evening and the next day… up until the funeral, which will begin at 2 p.m. tomorrow. It's an Orthodox tradition not to leave the departed one's body alone. We do what we can to honor this tradition, and the person's body, made sacred by the Incarnation.

After the interment at the cemetery, a "mercy meal" will be served back at the church. Long before her death, Urania made the arrangements… for Greek-style fish and vegetables to be catered. The "church ladies" will bring desserts.

Hugs are as plenteous as tears tonight, and my dear friend Nancy says to me, "What will we do without her?" She's referring, I'm sure, not only to her love and inspiration, but her matriarchal place among us… teaching us how to live.

"I guess we'll have to grow up now." The words are out before I can stop them. But there it is—the truth about losing mothers. It's our turn now. But these are big shoes to fill. By God's grace, we will grow into them. We are all changed forever by knowing her.

A few weeks after Urania's death and burial, her out of town family members fly in for the traditional forty-day memorial service. As they arrive at the church just before the Divine Liturgy on a Sunday morning in November, they file into the pew where she always sat. Her sons and daughters and even a cousin are there. Several times during the service, I find myself looking across the aisle at her place. In fact, I realize that I've been doing this every time I'm at church since she died. Sometimes I cry. Other times I smile. But, always, I'm still *watching*.

Hitting the Wall
2010

On the wall just outside the entrance to the Mississippi Sports Hall of Fame and Museum in Jackson, Mississippi, there's a single monument dedicated to my father—the man known as "The Guru of Running" in Mississippi. Etched in marble, the image of 67-year-old Bill Johnson, wearing a Mississippi State University baseball cap and a white running singlet, stands above the names of the winners of the "Watermelon 5K," the race that he founded in 1982. Under his name are the dates of his birth and death: January 20, 1930—July 9, 1998.

Even seasoned marathon runners often experience "hitting the wall" around mile 20 of the 26.219-mile race. Dad taught the runners he mentored during his career about this experience, explaining how the body runs out of chemical energy and the runner can suddenly feel as though his shoes are full of lead. He was able to avoid this during many of the marathons he ran, by proper nutrition and training.

My father's athletic career didn't begin with running. At Mississippi State University in the late '40s and early '50s he was the starting pitcher on the baseball team and also lettered in golf and basketball. After a brief stint on a farm league in Florida in the late '40s, he gave up baseball and became a championship level golfer, winning the City of Jackson and numerous country club invitationals throughout the state during the '50s and '60s. When he could no longer play scratch golf, (always shooting par or better) he turned in his cleats for running shoes. Dad had been a smoker for 25 years, and after quitting in the early '70s, he knew he needed to do something to keep the weight off. Both his parents had died of heart attacks, so Dad set out on a path of low-fat eating and intensive aerobic exercise.

He traded his two-martini business lunches for noonday runs with a group of men at the YMCA. This was before the running craze hit, so everyone said they were "hog wild" about running, and they eventually became known as the "Hog Wilds" and even had running shirts printed with that insignia. By the end of the '70s Dad was running 5Ks, 10Ks, and even marathons. He was only fifty-two years old when he retired from the life insurance business and opened "Bill Johnson's Phidippides Sports," a retail business specializing in athletic shoes, clothes, and informal training advice.

Life was good for Bill Johnson for the next fifteen years. From 1982 to 1997 he enjoyed a healthy lifestyle and a successful business. He ran all the big marathons, like Boston and New York, several times. One year he even competed in a triathlon. All this after age 50. Wanting to include the family, he built an aerobic dance studio adjacent to his store, which my mother oversaw. I taught aerobics there from 1982 until 1988, when I moved away from Jackson, and those were without a doubt the healthiest years of my life. To say Dad was a positive role model to those around him would be an understatement. Six-foot-two, with a slim runner's body, sky blue eyes and a mischievously dimpled smile (he always reminded me of Clint Eastwood), he seemed invincible. But all that changed abruptly in 1997.

Well, it actually started changing in 1995, when Dad first told his physician that he felt something strange, a twinge when he took a deep breath. Early chest x-rays showed a small, vague, gray area, but the bronchoscopy and needle biopsy were negative, so the doctors weren't concerned. But a life-long athlete is so attuned to his body that he can pick up signs others miss, so Dad went back again and again, asking for more x-rays. By 1997 the gray area proved to be a malignant tumor, bigger than any wall he had ever hit running marathons.

The next fourteen months were trying times for our family. Dad went into the hospital on May 13, 1997, expecting to have only one lobe of his right lung removed. During the surgery, a 4.5-centimeter adenocarcinoma with metastatic disease was found in one lobe, with involvement of a lymph node. A 5-millimeter lesion was discovered in another lobe, which also had metastasized. Additionally, a third tumor "of long duration" was found. The surgeon performed a pneumonectomy—the removal of his entire right lung—but unfortunately he wasn't able to completely eradicate the metastatic process that had begun to invade Dad's body.

Bill Johnson entered surgery a seasoned athlete and came out a semi-invalid. He would never again drive a car. In a few months he would no longer be able to take slow walks around an indoor track. He would become confined to a wheelchair and would require a portable oxygen tank at all times. Most people would have caved under such an emotional glycogen depletion, but Dad's training as a runner, combined with the community's image of him as hero—not only in athletics, but also in the spiritual and civic worlds—kept him from bonking at the twenty-mile marker of his final marathon, his race against death.

What he didn't know then was that some of the recommendations made by his physicians were futile attempts at prolonging the inevitable. Maybe they saw my father as an excellent candidate for experimental drugs because of his physical and spiritual strength. Maybe his physicians were urged on to prolong his life, even at the cost of greater suffering on Dad's part, because of the community hero status that he had acquired. Whatever their reasons, a year after the surgery, Dad's body was buckling under the weight of the hero's burden he'd been carrying most of his adult life. He suffered anxiety, hot flashes, weight loss, fever, chills, infections, depression, panic attacks, nausea, extreme confusion, and a severe allergic reaction to one of the chemotherapy drugs.

On one of my visits from Memphis, I drove Mom and Dad to the oncologist's office for his first chemotherapy treatment. The nurses greeted us with an air of hopeful enthusiasm. Once the blood work was done and Dad was set up in his recliner chair, the first round of Taxol began to drip into his veins from the bag hanging above his head. Mom and I pulled up chairs to keep him company, but in less than a minute Dad's face turned bright red and he began gasping for air. The room quickly filled with medical personnel and I heard someone say, "Page the doctor!" They unhooked the IV, administered oxygen and gave him an injection of some sort. Color returned to his face and we all began to breathe again, as if all the air had left the room and returned just as suddenly.

"Taxol is a fairly new drug," the doctor explained when he arrived. "We were hoping for a breakthrough, but Bill had a rare allergic reaction to it, so we're going to use Carboplatin and Navelbine."

That was in August of 1997. He received four full months of this cocktail. The physician's notes from a follow-up visit in January of 1998 reported, "his tolerance for this was good." But the notes also revealed that Dad had anxiety and hot flashes, and was seen in the emergency room in October for fever and chills. A large nodule in the left lung was thought to be pneumonia, and a splattering of small nodules was also present. The radiologist "thought there were more small nodules in the left lung than before and that some of these had increased in size." But the oncologist reviewed the CT scans and noted that they were performed at different intervals, which could have accounted for an appearance of growth in size.

It was difficult to get straight answers, and I often felt, during this time, that the oncologist wasn't completely transparent with my parents. But I was 200 miles away, and my parents were intelligent and capable of asking questions themselves. *Weren't they?* Years later, as I read the following paragraph near the end of the doctor's notes from that January visit, I regret that I wasn't more involved in the early stages of Dad's treatment:

"I discussed these findings with Mr. and Mrs. Johnson today. I told him that I did not think that we needed to intervene at this time. If this is metastatic disease, then subsequent follow-up will be able to verify this. These lesions are too small to biopsy now. Clinically he is doing well and does not have symptoms to suggest progression."

If this is metastatic disease? The first paragraph of the report stated that the surgery done the previous May revealed "intrapulmonary metastatic disease." *Wasn't that the reason for the four tortuous months of chemotherapy?* The notes did not indicate that any end-of-life discussion took place with my parents on that visit. Instead, they mentioned TB skin tests, steroid therapy and testosterone shots. While I was grateful that the physician had seemed to be treating Dad's physical condition as a whole, I was disturbed by his apparent lack of directness concerning Dad's prognosis. Mom and Dad seemed to have been left to their own intuition. At some point Dad expressed regret for having gone through the chemotherapy, saying that the "cure"—which was not really a cure—was worse than the disease. He wondered what the quality of the final year of his life might have been like had he chosen a different path. What if he had been counseled differently about his options? What if he had not allowed his body to be shot through with poisonous chemicals all those months? But it was too late for "what ifs." It was time to face the inevitable.

Mom was Dad's primary caregiver, with help from friends and neighbors who took turns staying with Dad while Mom ran errands or took a much-needed break for herself from time to time. At some point during those fourteen months, on one of my frequent visits from Memphis, the three of us sat down to talk about end-of-life issues. Mom and I went to the funeral home to make all the arrangements, and Dad made his wishes clear to us in his Durable Power of Attorney for Health Care. He wanted no "extreme measures" near the end. He wanted to die at home, with help from hospice staff. My parents didn't show their emotions very often, but on that day, Dad could barely say the words aloud without choking up, and Mom and I were swallowing our tears as we held our caregivers' smiles intact.

I was so glad when Dad decided to quit chemo. The physical race was over. It was time to gather emotional and spiritual resources for the most important and difficult leg of the marathon. It was time to get over the wall. What the three of us shared during the final week of my father's life was the best and worst that we can know in this life. We labored through the days and suffered through the nights, touching heaven and earth simultaneously.

I watched my parents' marriage of forty-nine years turn on its head under the stress of my father's impending death. With all the distractions removed—business, church, running, travel, civic and social engagements—they were left face to face with their brokenness. Fortunately, they had soft hearts, a strong faith, and an enduring love. I watched as their frustration and anger leaked out. Then I watched with admiration at the reconciliation and forgiveness that followed those moments of raw truth and emotion. One night I went into the living room and found them holding hands and crying.

"What's wrong?"

Dad managed a weak smile. "Your mother has been such an angel all these months, and I haven't been an easy patient. I've been irritable and hard to please, and it finally got to her."

I looked at Mother as she wiped her eyes and blew her nose

while getting up to find more tissues.

"Mother?"

"Oh, he hasn't been a bad patient. I'm just tired is all."

But Dad wanted me to understand. "I've asked her to forgive me and she feels guilty, but she's only human. If the tables had been turned and she had been the one who was sick, I could never have taken this good care of her."

It was more emotional intimacy than I had ever seen them share in my forty-seven years as their daughter. My tears mingled with theirs as the three of us held hands and prayed together. As I returned to Memphis from that visit, I had a sense that the end was near, and it was hard to leave them.

They met with the hospice social worker the following week, and she helped them get set up with a hospital bed, portable toilet, and other supplies they would need. She shared with them the hospice philosophy for end-of-life care, and left them a booklet to read, which Mom shared with me when I returned to Jackson for what would be the final week of Dad's life. The literature was excellent. We learned that hospice is a philosophy of care with a completely different approach than most of the cure-focused healthcare system. The hospice philosophy embraces death as a natural part of living, instead of something to always fight against. It's all about comfort and pain relief for the dying, and doesn't seek to either prolong life or hasten death. I was better able to wrap my head around the concept of "letting go" than Mom was, so she took a step back and asked me to take over as primary caregiver for those final days.

I think one of the most difficult things for family members to accept—especially for a wife who has been cooking for her husband for almost fifty years—is the patient's decreasing appetite. What southern woman, or any woman for that matter, doesn't associate cooking and feeding with nurturing and loving? So, when Dad began to refuse to eat, I reminded Mom what the social worker had told us, that he was being fed by the angels as he moved away from earth and towards heaven. He no longer needed earthly food, and his transition from earth to heaven would go more smoothly if we would embrace the process and not hold onto him too tightly. As the cancer began to shut down his vital organs, it was difficult for him to even swallow the tiny bites of applesauce into which I mixed his morphine tablets after grinding them with the back of a spoon.

Lung cancer is a relentless monster that literally sucks the air from its victim's world, resulting in a feeling of perpetual suffocation that rivals the pain of the worst forms of bone cancer. Dad's body fought the monster with more vigor than most of its victims because he was a trained marathon runner. His heart was so strong that it literally refused to stop beating, for days and perhaps months after a less con-ditioned organ would have given up. The irony of his condition was a cause of spiritual and moral confusion for Dad. *He had done all the right things*—he had quit smoking, embraced a lifestyle of low-fat foods and running over fifty miles most weeks, and had continued to be a spiritu-al leader at his church and in the community. For the first time in his life, he was angry with God. He wrestled as Jacob had with the angel, until he finally allowed himself to collapse into God's arms. I witnessed this struggle with reverence, and with thankfulness for the time he had been given to prepare to meet the God he had loved and served for sixty-eight years.

Friends from the running community visited less often as they witnessed his decline. Their hero had been reduced to an invalid in diapers, and it was more than they could bear to see. Elders from his church came on Sunday nights to anoint him with oil and to pray for his healing. When no apparent miracle arrived, their visits also decreased. When a colleague from Dad's former business firm arrived with his wife, just a few days before Dad's death, they broke down in tears at the sight of this fallen giant of their community. I had been especially close to this couple, having babysat for their children many years earlier, and so I encouraged them to spend some time talking with Dad. They shook their heads and apologized. They just couldn't do it.

My brother had been estranged from our family for many years, but as it became obvious that Dad had only a few days to live, we summoned him for a reconciliatory visit. As he asked for forgiveness and was received into his father's embrace, images of the Prodigal Son flooded my heart. Here was yet another reason to be thankful for this time of preparation, as painful as it was for Dad, and for all of us. We might think we would prefer a sudden death and the avoidance of suffering, but suffering offers opportunities for redemption. Hospice care provides the venue. It's up to the dying and their loved ones to take advantage of this unique setting.

As Dad's anxiety increased, he found it insufferable to lie in bed. He wanted to get up and walk around, which took great physical support from his caregivers. Mom and I hired sitters to relieve us from 11 p.m. to 7 a.m. so that we could sleep, but my ears were so tuned to Dad's voice that I often found myself running down the hall in the middle of the night, afraid that I would miss his passing. One night, after we had helped Dad get up and take a few labored steps—his arms around each of our shoulders for support—we put him back in the hospital bed, only to have him ask to get up again immediately. He was over six feet tall, and although he was a mere shadow of his former self, my back was screaming with pain and my emotions were raw and sleep-deprived. After hours of these repetitive transports from bed to floor and back to bed, my strength failed. I crawled onto the bed beside him and physically restrained him with my arm. I cried. I sang to him. I prayed aloud. I played his favorite music on a tape recorder we had set up beside his bed. But he cried out with all the strength he had left, "Please let me up. I can't breathe."

I asked if he wanted me to give him more morphine so that he could sleep and he whispered, "yes."

"You might not wake up if I do this, Dad. You might not be able to talk with us any more. Are you ready for that?"

His answer was clear. "Yes."

It was early morning and I called the hospice nurse to ask for permission to increase the morphine dose. She said she would have to ask the doctor. It seemed like an eternity before she called back with the news: the doctor wouldn't allow the dose to be increased. He said he would come by later that day to see Dad first. *Later that day?* The nurse understood my urgency and candidly encouraged me to find another physician to sign the orders, saying that Dad's physician had a reputation for not cooperating with hospice.

First I called the current doctor, who validated what the nurse had told me. He would not allow the hospice nurses the authority to increase medications as needed. "They are only nurses. They are not physicians."

"But they are the ones who are here with us," I protested. "They are the ones taking care of my father! You don't know what it's like. You don't see how he is suffering. You are not *here*!"

In that moment I was no longer the child. I became the adult my parents needed me to be. I fired the doctor over the phone, called another doctor—a dear friend from my parents' church, who had also seen Dad in his pulmonary practice during the past three years—and asked him to sign the paperwork, allowing the hospice nurse to increase Dad's meds. He took care of it immediately, and the hospice nurse called and said for me to increase the morphine. The doctor also said he would drop by to see Dad in an hour or two, which he did.

At this point you might be thinking, what prevented me from making the decision to increase the dose on my own? I thought about it, more than once. No one would have known, and I could have spared myself—and more importantly, my father—several more hours of suffering. But it wasn't that simple.

I was torn between the immediacy of Dad's discomfort and the moral implications of my actions. Mom had pretty much checked out, emotionally, by that point, so I was alone with the decision. Even with the new doctor's orders to increase the morphine, I was plagued with guilt and ambivalence. Would I be shortening my father's life?

The literature wasn't clear on this issue. Eleven years later a front-page article in *The New York Times* (December 27, 2009) chronicled the ethical, medical and emotional struggles of several terminally ill patients and their family members. "Hard Choice for a More Comfortable Death: Drug-Induced Sleep," by Anemona Hartocollis, introduced terminology like "terminal sedation" and "palliative sedation" to the general public. One of the physicians Hartocollis interviewed, Dr. Edward Halbridge, medical director at Franklin Hospital in Valley Stream on Long Island, was asked whether the meds that rendered his 88-year-old patient unconscious might have accelerated his death. "I don't know. He could have just been ready at that time."

Another physician, Dr. Lauren Shaiova, chairman of pain medicine and palliative care at Metropolitan Hospital Center in East Harlem, has drafted a twenty-page document with guidelines for palliative sedation. Seeking even more clarity in an area ridden with ambiguity, Dr. Paul Rousseau contributed an editorial to the *Journal of Palliative Medicine* in 2003—while he was a geriatrician with Veterans Affairs in Phoenix, Arizona—calling for more systematic research and guidelines.

His work noted different degrees of palliative sedation, including a level termed "intermittent deep sleep."

Hartocollis' article referenced several more physicians and spotlighted numerous personal stories to illustrate the complex issues at stake. A capstone, for me, was learning that in 2008, the American Medical Association issued a statement of support for palliative sedation, after the American Academy of Hospice and Palliative Medicine condoned "palliative sedation to unconsciousness."

As I read this comprehensive article in the midst of penning the story of my father's death many years later, I wondered if the decision I made in July of 1998 would have been any easier—or different—had this information been available at the time. Left alone with only my conscience as my guide, I made two phone calls.

First, I called my husband—a preventive medicine specialist who also happens to be an ordained Orthodox priest. And then I phoned my own spiritual confessor, the pastor at St. John Orthodox Church in Memphis. Neither of them could—or *would*—tell me what to do. I think they both sensed that there might not be a "right thing" to do in this situation. And so the two men whose love and wisdom I trusted most in the world were silent. Somehow I found the strength to push through the silence. I hung up the phone, asked God for mercy, and walked into the kitchen to prepare what would probably be the last dose of medicine my father would be able to swallow.

Mother went to her room, postponing the reality as long as possible, I think. Worried that Dad wouldn't be able to swallow the larger dose, I used as little applesauce as possible, working like an artist, grinding pigments with pestle and mortar until they slid smoothly from brush to canvas. Alone with Dad in the living room, I told him that the doctor had given permission for a larger dose. He nodded. I reminded him that he might not wake up. Did he want me to get Mom? Again he nodded. First I helped with the medicine, which took two or three tries before he finished the full dose. And then I wiped his mouth gently and walked down the hall to Mother's bedroom.

We returned together, and I witnessed my parents' final conversation in this life. A few minutes later, Dad closed his eyes and went to sleep.

The hospice nurse came by later, as did the physician, and each of them assured me that Dad was resting peacefully and was not in any distress. My instructions were, "If he wakes again, give him another dose of the morphine."

When the sitter arrived for the night shift, Dad hadn't moved, but his breathing was steady, so Mom and I opted for a few hours of sleep. Early the next morning the sitter knocked on the door to the room where I was sleeping. "Mrs. Cushman, I think you and your mother should come be with him now."

I flew out of bed, pausing briefly to call to Mom through the open door of her room, and she followed me quickly into the living room. Once we were at Dad's side, the sitter slipped quietly into the kitchen, allowing us privacy with Dad. Her hospice training had taught her that the ragged breaths he was drawing were signs that the end was near. We had read in the hospice literature that sometimes a dying person experiences a final surge of alertness and energy, just before the end, and we didn't want to miss it. As we stood, and later sat, on either side of his bed, he slept through much of his final morning. And then it happened.

Early on the afternoon of July 9, Dad woke briefly from his coma-like sleep, smiled, and made eye contact with Mom and me for the first time in twenty-four hours.

"I love you, Daddy."

Mother could barely find her voice. "I love you, sweetie."

"It's okay, Dad. I'll take care of Mother. You can go now."

He responded to our words by squeezing our hands. And then he was gone—the most powerful sunset I have ever seen.

As we stood there holding his hands, I was struck by the complexity of my grief, which was infused with an uneasy mixture of relief and exhaustion. But then my mother's pain, which she had contained for fourteen months, poured from her mouth like the sounds of a woman in childbirth as she collapsed onto Dad's chest. I ran around to her side of the bed to support her, and we stood there for a long time, weeping. Finally I reached for my little red Orthodox prayer book and began to read the Prayer at the Death of a Parent. Mother regained her strength and joined me as we read together the Prayer at the Death of a Spouse. And then we read the 23rd Psalm, which was Dad's favorite. I had visions of him running past the twenty-mile marker as we read the fourth verse: "And yea though I walk through the valley of the shadow of death, I will fear no evil."

Walker, Alzheimer's, and Sunset Park
(Excerpt from Chapter 8, *John and Mary Margaret*, 2021)

Mary Margaret loved theater and she and Walker had season tickets to the Memphis Symphony Orchestra and the Orpheum Theater, which were both downtown. After enjoying many performances at both venues over the years, Mary Margaret approached Walker about an idea she had been mulling over in her mind. It was 2009, and "The Color Purple" was playing at The Orpheum. Their tickets were for the Saturday afternoon matinee.

"Hey, Walker, how would you like to get away somewhere pretty and relaxing this weekend, without having to drive more than thirty minutes?"

"Is this a trick question? And I thought we had tickets for a play at The Orpheum this weekend."

"No. And yes." Mary Margaret laughed. "I mean no, it's not a trick question, and yes we do have tickets for The Orpheum. So, I thought maybe we could spend the weekend in that boutique hotel on Mud Island—you know, the one right at the entrance to Harbor Town? We could get a room with a view of the Mississippi River, sleep in both mornings, and enjoy dinner at the restaurant downstairs from our room. There's also a great coffee shop just down the street, and a casual bar and grill next door. How does that sound?"

"That sounds like you've been planning this for a while." Walker smiled. "But it actually sounds like a good idea. Have you already booked our room?"

"Oh, you know me well, don't you? It's a suite. And the hotel is only about five minutes from The Orpheum. We could drive or take a cab."

The weekend was everything Mary Margaret had envisioned, and more. On Sunday afternoon, after checking out of the hotel, they drove north on Island Drive to explore the "island"—which was really a peninsula—a bit more. Lots of people were walking, jogging, and riding bikes along the river. Near the end of the waterfront, just as the road took a ninety-degree right turn, back towards the city, Mary Margaret noticed a large building facing the river. The sign out front said, "Sunset Park Senior Living."

"Huh. I didn't know there was a senior living facility down here, did you?" Mary Margaret asked Walker, who glanced out the window as he continued to drive.

"Yes, I heard they were building one. Didn't know it was finished. Does it look nice?"

"I couldn't get a good look, but wow, what a location! Right here on the river. I guess it's good to know about it in case either of us needs a place like this one day."

"One day" came sooner than they expected, as Walker began to show symptoms of cognitive decline—both at work and at home.

"Where's the—what do you call that thing?" He said to Margaret one Saturday, walking around the den, looking under a stack of newspapers and behind the cushion in his recliner.

"What thing, dear?"

"You know, the little thing that you use to turn the TV on and change the channels."

Mary Margaret looked up from the book she was reading. "You mean the remote? It's over there on the coffee table."

"Damn it," Walker said, picking up the remote and pointing it at the television.

"Why are you so upset? It wasn't even lost."

"It's not that I couldn't find the remote . . . it's that I couldn't remember what it's called. Happens all the time lately. The other day at work I couldn't remember what to call a calculator."

"Oh, honey, that happens to all of us. I wouldn't worry about it."

But as the months and years went by, Walker's memory loss became more obvious. He began to forget how to do simple tasks, like making coffee or using his electric shaver. He and Mary Margaret would be having a conversation and he would just stop in the middle of a sentence . . . searching in vain for the words.

Finally, in 2010, he sold the business to two of his younger managers, and he and Mary Margaret made a move that surprised their daughters. They bought one of those stately homes right on the river in Harbor town. Ever the cautionary older daughter, Emily was the first to express her concerns.

"What are you thinking, Mom?" she asked on a weekend visit from Oxford. Don't most people scale down when they retire? And all your friends are out east. You will be a half hour from most of the people you know."

"Let's go for a drive," Mary Margaret said. "I want to show you something."

As they drove from Mary Margaret and Walker's home in East Memphis, through Midtown, and finally over the bridge onto Mud Island, Mary Margaret reminded her daughter of all the things she and Walker enjoyed downtown—the symphony, The Orpheum Theater, and so many nice restaurants. And then she turned onto Island Drive.

"Okay, I know it's beautiful here," Emily said. "And yes, these houses are amazing."

She turned into the first entrance to the neighborhood and pointed out the restaurants, coffee shop, boutique grocery store, 24-hour fitness center, dry cleaners, and nail salon all on one block. "We can walk to these places, or ride a golf cart." She laughed as a woman parked her golf cart in front of the fitness center and hopped out with her yoga mat in one hand and a water bottle in the other.

As they continued through the neighborhood with its winding streets, sidewalks, and numerous parks and duck ponds, Emily began to see what drew her mother to the place. But then Mary Margaret turned back out onto Island Drive and continued north, past the neighborhood and a couple of apartment complexes, until they arrived at Sunset Park. She pulled into the drive and stopped in front of the main building.

Emily looked at the sign and then at her mother. "So, what's this? You and dad are only in your sixties. Are ya'll moving into a senior living facility?"

"No. But I want to be close to one for when—for when I can't take care of your father at home. This would be just down the street from our house."

Emily's eyes filled with tears. "Oh, Mom, I didn't realize it was getting that bad. I can totally see why this is a good idea. And you're still just over an hour from my place in Oxford."

They joined a bridge club, and even took up golf. Their friends in the bridge club were the first to comment on Walker's decline. "It's not that he can't remember which cards have been played," one of them said after an evening of cards. "It's that he doesn't even remember how the game is played." That was the end of that social outlet.

Golf lasted a bit longer, as his muscle memory kicked in when he picked up a club and swung at the ball. But Mary Margaret found herself telling him which club to use for each shot, when it had always been the other way around. A diagnosis of Alzheimer's confirmed their suspicions, and their "sunset years" were more like one long, slow, climb backwards down a steep cliff.

As Walker's cognitive abilities declined, he also became frustrated and sometimes belligerent towards Mary Margaret. Embarrassed by his incontinence and angry about his loss of control—both mentally and physically—he lashed out at the people she hired to help with his care, and often at Mary Margaret herself. Returning from her writing group meeting one day several years into his decline, she found him screaming at the aide who was trying to help him back into his bed for a nap.

"Walker!" Mary Margaret hurried into the room. "Robert is just trying to help you."

"Robert?" Walker's face showed confusion and fear. "Who the hell is Robert?"

"It's me, Mr. Richardson," Robert said, "I've been taking care of you today, and lots of days before this."

"Have you given him a sedative?" Mary Margaret asked.

"No, ma'am. He wouldn't take it. Pushed it out of my hand and threw the glass of water across the room."

Mary Margaret looked at the broken glass on the floor near the window, and back at Walker, who was still sitting up on the edge of the bed. "Honey, let's lay down for a little rest now, okay? I'll get you a nice glass of juice and something to help you feel better."

She was able to get Walker to take the sedative that day, and when he finally fell asleep, she fell apart at the kitchen table. Robert joined her, bringing them both a cup of coffee.

"How long have you been taking care of Alzheimer's patients, Robert?" Mary Margaret asked.

"Long time, Mrs. Richardson. Probably twenty years or more."

"So, you've seen this before, these outbursts?"

"Sure, plenty of times. It just comes with the disease. He doesn't mean anything by it."

"Oh, I know that. It's not that I'm taking it personally. It's just that—well, I wonder how long I can handle having him here." Tears filled her eyes. "Do you think it's time for me to put him in a facillity?"

"That's a decision for you and your doctor to make, ma'am. Some people can keep their loved ones at home 'til the end, but some just need more help. And sometimes it's actually a blessing for people in Mr. Richardson's condition to be in a place where he's safe and all his needs are met."

"You sound like you're speaking from experience, Robert."

"Yes, ma'am. I worked at a couple of those places for years before doing in-home care. You know, one of the best places for that happens to be right down the road from your house. Have you seen Sunset Park? You could visit and see what you think."

Sunset Park's long-term care center turned out to be a God-send for Walker, and Mary Margaret. At first she felt guilty for putting him there—that was in 2012—but as time went by and cruelly erased his memory of her, she noticed that he seemed happy in his new world. He was always smiling when she visited, especially when his favorite aide would walk into the room.

"Oh, Mr. Walker, look who's here to see you today! Your beautiful bride!"

His eyes would light up, but Margaret could tell that he was responding more to the presence of the aide than to her. At first that hurt her feelings, and she had to keep reminding herself that it was the disease that caused Walker to forget her. She could only handle spending an hour or two with him each day—and the social worker at the home even said that was the recommended amount of time for visits with Alzheimer's patients. She didn't know whether she said that because it was true or just to make Mary Margaret feel better, but somehow it freed her to spend more time doing things in the community. In addition to the writing group she had joined, she found a women's bridge club and a book club. And a wonderful "gentle yoga" class for seniors.

The hardest times were the evenings, alone in their home. She had just read *The Hours* by Michael Cunningham, and often found herself bemoaning "the hours" before her, as she wondered how much longer Walker would live, and what she might do with the rest of her years. She had been keeping a journal since the beginning of Walker's illness, and she began writing a memoir. As she shared chapters of it with her writing group, they encouraged her to keep going, and to consider publishing it one day. Maybe, she thought. After Walker . . . after he's gone.

Elizabeth and Lewy Body Dementia
(Excerpt from Chapter 9, *John and Mary Margaret*)

After Elizabeth retired from Porter-Leath in 2013, she was restless at home alone. John was still busy with work, and Elizabeth had never had much "free time" during her career. Working full time for forty years hadn't allowed much time for socializing with friends, and her sons were busy with their own careers.

She volunteered one day a week with the Memphis Child Advocacy Center, which served children who were victims of sexual or physical abuse. Otherwise, she spent a lot of time at home, trying to figure out what to do next. As the months went by, she felt more and more distant from the world around her. Everything began to feel "fuzzy."

One day when John came home from work, he found Elizabeth sitting at the kitchen table staring at a cookbook. Pots and pans were strewn around the kitchen, some on the cabinets and others on the floor, along with measuring cups and spoons. A package of frozen chicken breasts was sitting on the counter near the refrigerator, along with a few onions and a bag of potatoes. It was almost 5:30 p.m., and Elizabeth was still in her nightgown and robe, which was uncharacteristic for her. As John walked in the door, she looked up from the table and burst into tears.

John put down his briefcase and moved to the chair beside her, putting his arm around her shoulders. "What's all this?" he asked, looking around at the cluttered kitchen. "Are you writing a cookbook?" His tone was light, but he sensed that something was wrong with Elizabeth.

"Oh, John, I don't know what's wrong, but I just can't think clearly. I was going to cook some chicken for supper, but . . . ." She covered her face with her hands and wept loudly.

"But, what, dear?" John pulled her into his arms for an embrace.

Once she caught her breath, she looked at John with fear in her eyes. "Something is wrong with me, John. My brain—it just isn't working right. I can't figure out this simple recipe. And the chicken is hard as a rock."

John looked at the chicken breasts, still in their plastic wrap on the counter. "Well, they're frozen. Does the recipe call for them to be thawed first?" His tone was kind, not judgmental, but Elizabeth wasn't comforted.

"I don't know what the damn recipe says, John. I can't . . . I can't read it. The words don't make sense. And when I got the pots and pans out of the cabinet, I dropped some of them on the floor. My hands just wouldn't hold onto them." She held up her hands with the palms towards her face. They were shaking.

Fear gripped John and his mind raced to drastic considerations. Did she have Parkinson's? Was she having a stroke? He rushed to the phone to call their physician. It was after hours and he got the answering service. "If this is an emergency, please dial 911."

Was this an emergency? Not knowing what else to do, he dialed 911 and explained what was happening. "If your wife isn't in urgent need of care, I suggest you make an appointment with her physician, but if you don't think it can wait, you should drive her to a nearby emergency room." He considered what constituted an emergency—chest pain, numbness in her arms, blurry vision, all signs of a stroke or heart attack—but Elizabeth didn't seem to have any of these. He decided to wait and call her physician the next day.

The following months were excruciating, as John took Elizabeth to one doctor after another—including a trip to Mayo Clinic, where she finally received a diagnosis. Elizabeth had Lewy Body Dementia. Some of Elizabeth's symptoms, like muscle problems and tremors, were similar to Parkinson's, which is one reason the disease is often misdiagnosed. She was only sixty-three years old. Unlike Alzheimer's, which more often affects older people, Lewy Body frequently strikes younger victims, and the life expectancy is also shorter. The doctors told her she probably wouldn't make it to seventy.

Devastated by the news, John and Elizabeth set out to do everything they could. They traveled to Europe—something Elizabeth had always dreamed about. She needed help with mobility, and eventually even a wheelchair. Back home they made changes to accommodate her diminishing motor skills. John had a hospital bed set up in the sun room near the kitchen when Elizabeth could no longer handle the stairs leading up to their bedroom. Eventually John hired home healthcare aides to be with Elizabeth when he was working. Finally he retired from his position as General Sessions Judge in 2015, but even with him being home full time and with outside help, Elizabeth's care became too much. It was time to consider moving her to a facility, which broke his heart. Elizabeth could barely communicate with words at that point, but her eyes told him she was still there. When he told her about the potential move, she nodded, with tears.

John researched all the long-term care facilities in Memphis, and finally decided on a place on the north end of Mud Island. He could drive there in thirty minutes from their home on South Parkway, and it was close to his son Martin's law office downtown, so Martin would be able to visit easily. His friends wondered why he didn't choose one of the nursing homes in East Memphis, closer to his house. They hadn't seen the view at Sunset Park.

Father Basil and Susan on boat
to Aegina, Greece 2007

Susan's granddaughters, to whom she dedicated her novel *John and Mary Margaret*

Susan with her mother,
Effie Johnson, 2007

"The Littlest Sweeheart" with brother,
Mike, and parents, Bill and Effie
Johnson

Susan with her father,
Bill Johnson, 1988

"The Littlest Sweetheart,"
Jackson, Mississippi, 1960

"Weeping" icon of St. Mary of
Egypt (Detail from the author's
original icon. "Tears"
added by See Cushman using
Photoshop. This image appears
on the back cover of
Susan's first novel, *Cherry Bomb*.)

Mother of God, Directress, for
the nave at St. John Orthodox
Church, Memphis

"Wedding Icon" of Sts. Basil the Great
and Mary of Egypt (all icons by the
author)

Christ , "Extreme Humility"

Susan working on icon of
St. John

Susan finishing details on Icon
of Christ the Lightgiver

"Wide Margins," original poem
illustrated with gouache

Christ the Lightgiver, for the nave
at St. John Orthodox Church,
Memphis

IV

Family and Adoption

I remember all the times our best friends had babies. We would hurry to see them in the hospital, taking flowers or balloons and smiling and celebrating with each of them. And then I would cry my eyes out on the ride home.

—Susan Cushman, *"Parenthood Redux"*

Her name is Kim Ei Soo. Jason had it painted in calligraphy on a colorful wall hanging he bought on his first trip to Korea. Along with his biological sister's name, Ahn Jong Hee. The banner hung in his room for a long time, a vivid expression of his longing and devotion.

—Susan Cushman, *"The Other Woman"*

The Littlest Sweetheart

(A chapter from an unpublished memoir, *Dressing the Part:*
What I Wore For Love)

1960. That was the year she got to wear her Easter dress more than once. Like every year she could remember before that, Susan's grandmother had made her dress. This year she had included a baby blue silk half slip that was designed to peek out just under the hem of the white eyelet dress. Her grandmother had even made a matching dress for one of her dolls with leftover fabric. The silk ribbon-tie belt was the perfect finishing touch, along with her white anklet socks with eyelet trim.

Her mother had put her hair up in pink foam-rubber curlers the night before. She had slept in them overnight, hoping her straight blonde hair would hold some of the curl just long enough for her appearance at the Choctaw Little League baseball game that night. They would be crowning the queen of the league, and she was one of the contestants, along with the other team sweethearts.

Her older brother's team—Jackson Ready-Mix—was coached by her father, and she had been chosen as team sweetheart earlier in the summer. It was her proudest moment. She loved wearing her sweetheart "uniform" to all the games: a white blouse with a red heart on the pocket, red short shorts, and a matching red baseball cap with a white heart and letter "C" for Choctaw League on front. Girls weren't allowed to play little league baseball in 1960, and Susan was actually a good pitcher. This was the closest she would get to wearing a baseball uniform.

She told herself that it didn't matter that the sweethearts of all the other teams were eleven or twelve, whereas she was only nine.

And it didn't matter than most of them had boyfriends on the team they represented. She tried to dismiss the thought that she had only been chosen because of her eleven-year-old brother and her father. But what she had the most difficult time dismissing was that some of the other sweethearts already had breasts. Susan had asked her mother for a training bra to wear with her new dress. She had secret plans to stuff it with two of her ankle socks. But her mother had declined, saying that she was too young for a bra.

Finally it was time for the ceremony, which would take place just before that night's game. She was escorted onto the field by her brother, followed by her father and mother. She eyed the other sweethearts, some of whom had fancy "up dos" for their hair. Susan's hair was short and swept to one side on top and held with a white bow. She was relieved to see that the older girls were also wearing short dresses, probably because it was July in Jackson, Mississippi, and it was too hot for a long dress outside. But then she saw their legs and feet. They were all wearing *stockings* with little white pumps. Heels! She looked down at her white patent leather Mary Janes and cringed. But then the ceremony began and she forgot all about those little white pumps.

The president of the league stood on the pitcher's mound, with all the sweethearts and their escorts spread out on either side of him. It was still light outside, so the electric lights hadn't been turned on yet. The president thanked everyone for their support of the league that summer, and especially for the teams who raised money to pay for the lights, mostly by selling candy. Finally he announced which team had raised the most money—Jackson Ready-Mix!

Susan's mother urged her to walk up to the pitcher's mound, just as the bat boy for Jackson Ready-Mix approached carrying a silk pillow with a crown on top. The only thing missing was music like they play at the Miss America pageant. But when the crown was placed on her head and she was declared to be Queen of the Choctaw Little League, all her doubts and concerns faded away. Her father and mother both kissed her and she thought she would cry. She briefly glanced at the older sweethearts who—to their credit—were clapping and wore pageant smiles—and thought she would burst. But the best part of all was when her brother hugged her and said, "I'm so proud of you, Sis."

She sat in the stands with her mother during the game that followed, barely noticing that her brother's team won, giving her family a second victory that night. All she could think about was how she couldn't wait to get home and write a letter to her grandmother, telling her all about the evening and how perfect the dress was.

Back home later that night, as she put away her dress, she said to her mother, "Just wait 'til next year."

"Next year?" her mother looked confused. "What could be better than being crowned Queen of the Choctaw Little League?"

Susan pulled her nightgown over her head and gave her mother a sly smile. "Well, being Queen was pretty nice, but next year maybe I can wear stockings and pumps . . . and a bra!"

Avery
(A story from *Friends of the Library*, a short story collection.)
2019

Arriving at the Lafayette County and Oxford Public Library felt more like being back on sorority row at Ole Miss. My mind was immediately flooded with memories of my time as a student at this school that has always been known for having the most beautiful girls in the South—or anywhere. I changed clothes several times before driving down to Oxford, finally settling on a conservative black pencil skirt and pink sweater set. My mother's pearls and matching pearl earrings gave me what I hoped was a professional but not-too-stuffy look.

The library's redbrick exterior and tall white columns were adorned with a huge banner hanging from the second-floor balcony that read, *ARE YOU READY?* As I walked from the parking lot to the door—adding an intentional spring to my step and sway to my hips—I half expected a group of students to come pouring out of their cars yelling the iconic Ole Miss cheer, "HELL, YEAH! DAMN STRAIGHT! HOTTY TODDY . . ."

Named for the university town of Oxford, England, our Oxford is home to the state's first university, which opened its doors in 1848. But Ole Miss isn't Oxford's only attraction. In addition to good food, quaint boutiques, and one of the nation's most famous bookstores—Square Books, home to the Thacker Mountain Radio show—Oxford hosts year-round sporting, literary, and musical events.

Each April it hosts the Oxford Conference for the Book and the Double Decker Festival. In June it provides the LOU Summer Sunset Series, the Oxford Film Festival, and the Yoknapatawpha Summer

Writers' Workshop. The annual Faulkner and Yoknapatawpha Conference is in July.

It was into this magical cultural milieu that I went to speak at the library's "Books and Lunch" gathering, where brown bag lunches were offered free to anyone who signed up for the reading. A nice crowd showed up to hear me read from my novel. My protagonist is a runaway orphan who throws up graffiti and ends up with a scholarship to Savannah College of Art and Design (SCAD). So, I hoped to see lots of college kids at the reading. But as often happens at these library events, the audience was comprised mostly of teachers and retired teachers. As I was about to start, a tall, lanky young man walked in and sat in the back row of the small auditorium.

I had met Avery at the front desk of the library when I first arrived. He worked part time while writing for a local newspaper, and—here comes the best part—working on a fantasy novel.

After talking about my novel and reading a few selections, I opened the floor for questions. I could almost write the script for the Q&A time after doing so many of these readings.

"How did you become interested in graffiti?" "Have you ever actually seen a weeping icon?" "Why did you decide to write a book about three women who were all sexually abused?"

Avery's questions revealed his writer's heart. "How did you decide which point of view to use? Did you consider writing in first person? Was it difficult to mix real life persons and places with the fictional ones?"

I answered each of his questions with clipped answers, not wanting to bore the non-writers in the room but hoping later to speak privately with Avery.

"So, how old are you, Avery?" I asked after everyone else had left and he was helping me pack up the books that didn't sell at the event.

"I'm twenty-six. I know what you're thinking. Why is someone my age working part time in a library?" His self-effacing demeanor added to his charm. Six feet and change, with wavy brown hair tucked behind his ears, his long legs barely filled out his skinny jeans, which were topped off with a T-shirt that read, *Divergent.*

"Well, actually, I was wondering if you were a student."

"No. I did a couple of years at community college, but I couldn't seem to focus. I really just wanted to write."

"I hear you. So, tell me about your fantasy novel. What interested you about that genre?"

"It's a long story. I don't want to take up too much of your time. I'm sure you need to get on the road or something."

"Actually, I was going to stop at Square Books before leaving town. Can you get away and join me on their balcony for a cup of coffee?"

Avery looked at his phone and then glanced out the door of the auditorium into the library.

"Let me see how busy we are. Maybe I can take a break."

Driving around the square in Oxford was like flashing back in time. Like other small towns in the South, it was built around a central structure—a town hall that anchors its grid. Covered sidewalks line the stores fronting on the circle. Square Books still maintains a historic sign attached to its terra-cotta stucco exterior that reads, *Fortune's Famous Ice Cream.*

Inside the bookstore, shelves were filled with a multitude of works by famous and up-and-coming authors, many of whom lived, or had once lived, in Oxford and other Mississippi towns. It was at once inspiring and intimidating to be surrounded by such genius, and also thrilling to see my own novel on the shelves with some of those brilliant Mississippi authors.

I visited briefly with one of the employees, found my way upstairs, grabbed a latte from the coffee bar, and headed out to the balcony. My feet were killing me, so I took off the black leather heels I had had chosen to wear, wishing I had opted for a comfy pair of sandals instead. In my mid-sixties, I still struggled to accept the limitations my aging body tried to put on my fashion sense.

Large green ferns hung in baskets above the balcony's railing. A breeze brought enticing smells from the nearby restaurant kitchens. The atmosphere was charged with memories of so many Saturday afternoons I had spent there in years past, when my writing group met monthly to critique each other's works in progress. It was still hard for me to believe that those chapters they helped me shape and the characters they helped bring to life on the pages of my novel were being read in this iconic bookstore. And now I was getting acquainted with a young writer starting on his own journey.

Avery found me outside a few minutes later and we sat in wicker chairs at one end of the balcony. He tossed his backpack on the table and looked at me expectantly. "Ms. Covington—you beat me here."

"Oh, please, Avery, call me Adele. It makes me feel much younger." I smiled as he blushed and ran his fingers through his hair. "And by the way, what's your last name?"

"Oh, that. It's Carmichael."

"So, you were going to tell me how you got interested in fantasy, Avery Carmichael." I smiled at his shyness and sipped my latte and watched as he seemed to consider his response.

"I started reading Robert Jordan's books when I was in high school. Especially the Conan the Barbarian series. But later I got into his Wheel of Time books. I loved being able to escape into a whole different world from the one I grew up in."

Avery's voice dropped off and he looked away.

"What was that world like?"

"Well, I was adopted when I was a baby. But my adoptive mom got pregnant right after they got me, so she had a biological son just a year younger than me."

"What was that like for you, growing up?"

"It was okay. I mean, they were nice to me and all that, but I never felt as close to my parents as my brother seemed to be. And I always felt like we were competing. But he was better at sports and was in the popular crowd and all that. I kind of gravitated towards the grunge kids. Got into drugs. My parents never had me tested, but I'm pretty sure I have ADD, so I was self-medicating with pot and other stuff." Avery paused long enough to light a cigarette and take a drink of his black coffee. "Do you mind if I smoke?"

"Not at all. That's what God made the fresh air for, right?" We both laughed, and I brought us back to the discussion at hand. "Tell me about your novel."

"It's kind of dystopian fantasy. Set in a future world where babies are warehoused away from their parents and then adopted out to couples they are matched with."

"Sounds like *The Handmaid's Tale*."

"It's got some similarities, only it's not a Christian theonomy like the one that overthrew the government in that book. It's more like a neo-Nazi society, where the government is trying to put the best babies with the best parents to raise super beings."

"Avery, why on earth would you want to escape to such a world? I thought you were creating fantasy to find a better life than the one you had growing up."

"I know it sounds weird, but here's the thing. The protag is a kid who leads a group of rebels who want to find their birth parents."

I got it. Avery and I sat quietly for a few minutes. I looked at my watch and realized I needed to start driving home. I wanted to leave Avery with some encouragement.

"I think you've got a great idea there. Have you had anyone read what you've written so far?"

Avery shook his head.

"Look, I know it's scary showing your stuff to others for the first time, but if you ever want to publish a book, you've got to get some help. How much have you written so far?"

"About twenty-five thousand words."

"That's a great start! Hey—I know about a workshop you might want to look into. It's called the Yoknapatawpha Summer Writers' Workshop, and it's here in Oxford every May or June. I went to it seven years in a row, and it really helped. Want me to send you a link to the workshop's website? Actually, I can give you an email for the guy who organizes it."

"Sure, why not?"

Avery picked up his backpack and held the door for me as we left the balcony and headed back downstairs and out the front door of the bookstore. Laughter wafted down from the balcony bar at City Grocery, two doors down. Locals and students came and went from the shops and bars and restaurants all around the square. I loved the creative spirit that seemed to permeate this little patch of literary heaven.

"Thanks for taking time to visit with me, Adele," Avery said as I got my sunglasses out of my purse and put them on for the drive home.

"It was my pleasure. Good luck with your book." I gave Avery a quick hug goodbye and headed home.

Three months later Avery drove onto the Ole Miss campus and pulled up to the Depot—the 150-year old facility that was declared a Mississippi landmark in 1992. Back in the 1870s, the Depot bustled with students, faculty and visitors. Mail trains delivered packages and letters from family and friends. William Faulkner, who served as the college's postmaster at one time, gathered sacks of mail from the depot and carried them to the university's post office. After much renovation, the building became available for use by groups of up to sixty people in 2003. One of those groups became the Yoknapatawpha Summer Writers' Workshop.

Organized and led by faculty members in the MFA creative writing program at Ole Miss and other universities, the workshop was a weekend gathering of about fifteen mostly new and emerging writers who submitted samples of their works in progress to be critiqued by the faculty and their fellow participants. Everyone received copies of each other's writing ahead of time, and students were asked to be prepared to offer feedback during the workshop as well as pass along written notes on each manuscript. In addition to the critique sessions, authors, editors, literary agents, and publicists gave craft talks during the weekend. And of course there were social events like a night at Taylor Grocery for catfish, and a reading at Square Books, usually for one of the authors on faculty for the workshop.

Avery worried about others seeing—and worse yet, critiquing—his words. But that's what the shy boy had signed up for, and on Saturday morning the time came for his piece to be *workshopped,* as the process was called. First the workshop leader, an MFA grad named Grant, asked Avery to make a few introductory comments about his writing sample. Just as he started, a middle-aged woman walked in and quietly sat in a chair at the back of the room.

"Oh, wait just a minute, Avery. Let me introduce one of our

speakers who has just arrived first. This is Julia Wilson, who teaches in the MFA program here at Ole Miss. Julia also has published several books of poetry, and she will be talking with us later this morning about how poetry affects prose in our first craft talk of the weekend. Welcome, Julia!"

Julia smiled and nodded. "Thanks, Grant. I didn't mean to interrupt. I promise to be quiet."

Grant laughed and indicated to Avery that he could give his introduction.

"It's a dystopian fantasy," Avery began. "The setting is somewhere in America in the future—maybe around the year 3,000. It's after a third world war, and the totalitarian government takes all newborn babies from their parents and puts them in warehouses until they are assigned to a new set of parents, with the most prominent members of society having first pick. Babies from lower-class birth parents are often left in the warehouses—which then become orphanages—and later trained to do mundane jobs. The protagonist, Balock, and his girlfriend, Ember, are leading a rebellion against the government, in order to stop this procedure and to find their birth parents. The manuscript I turned in is the opening chapter and—"

"Okay," Grant interrupted. He instructed Avery to stay quiet during his critique session, which would last about thirty minutes, and to take notes. Next, Grant gave a brief summary, commenting on how Avery was doing with world building and how the characters' stories connected emotionally with the reader. Then he opened up the floor to other participants.

Avery was asked about his choice to write in first-person present tense, and about his crafting of futuristic phrases, especially in the dialogue. Although Julia had promised to remain quiet, she piped up near the end of his session, complimenting his pacing and the lyrical quality of his writing.

"So, Avery, I was just wondering two things, actually. First of all, have you ever written poetry, or had any instruction in it? Your prose reflects a natural gift for rhythm. And the second question is why did you choose to write about a protagonist who was leading a crusade for himself and others to find their birth parents? There's such a strong emotional pull, even in this opening chapter."

Avery looked down at his laptop, on which he had taken notes during the critique session. He shifted nervously in his chair, clasped his hands together, and slowly looked up at Julia.

"Well, the first question is easy. I've always loved poetry—reading it and also writing a few mongrels myself, since I was a kid, really."

"Who did you read?" Julia asked.

"Mark Doty is a favorite. *Atlantis* was amazing. I also really like T. S. Eliot and Allen Ginsberg."

Julia nodded and waited for Avery to answer her second question.

"On the choice of my subject matter, that's really personal."

"Of course, you don't have to answer if you don't want to. But you should know that if you publish this book and give readings one day, people will probably ask you this same question. Readers often want to know what inspires authors' subjects. And if it's fiction, they want to know if any of the book is autobiographical."

Avery took a minute before answering. He looked at Grant, his eyes asking for a way out. Grant stepped in.

"She's got a point, Avery. But you seem uncomfortable with her question, so maybe you need to just sit with this for a while. Even reconsider if this is what you really want to write about. You could always—"

"Okay, so I was adopted. Is that what you wanted to know? Can't a person just write a book without everyone getting all up in his business?"

Avery slammed his laptop shut, tossed it into his backpack and left the room. He didn't want to miss Julia's craft talk, but he wasn't sure he could stand the way he was feeling one minute longer. Like someone was peeling off a layer of his skin.

He left the building and headed for his car, where he rolled down a window and lit a cigarette. He thought about dropping out of the workshop and just heading back to his apartment where he could hide out with his secrets. But everyone had been so encouraging about his book, about his writing. He had come here to learn how to be a writer, to make his book better, and he couldn't let his feelings interfere.

When he walked back into the Depot, everyone was milling around, getting another cup of coffee during the break. Julia was preparing for her presentation at the front of the room. Grant approached Avery and put his hand on his shoulder.

"Hey, man. I hope we didn't overstep back there. These workshops can get pretty intense. You okay?"

"Yeah, sure. I shouldn't have gone off like that. I guess I just wasn't prepared, emotionally, for how this would go."

"Just remember that it's your book. We're all just here to give you feedback. You decide what to do with it, kind of like what they say in twelve steps meetings; take what works and leave the rest."

Everyone found their seats and Grant stood to introduce Julia's craft talk. But first he made an announcement.

"Okay, everyone. It's time for our first craft talk of the weekend, but first I've got an announcement. One of our faculty members for the workshop just had a family emergency and had to cancel, so I invited Adele Covington, an author from Memphis, to come down and

give a talk in his place tomorrow. In fact, Adele just texted me that she's
almost here and will be joining us for this next session. Wait—here she
is now."

    I walked into the room and tried to duck quietly into a chair on
the back wall, but Grant saw me and introduced me. Everyone turned
around to the back of the room, and as I smiled and nodded, my eyes
caught a familiar face—Avery! He smiled and gave a slight wave.

    Julia handed out copies of excerpts from several works of
prose. She asked the class to compare the pieces, looking for good use
of rhythm and pacing in some, and economy of words in others. Next,
she led them through a free-write session that involved childhood memories. Several people shared what they had written, and they discussed
how to use those memories in their works in progress. Avery forgot
about his earlier discomfort and lost himself in the session, enthused
that he could apply the lessons to his own writing.

    "It's time for lunch," Grant announced after the talk was over.
"There are lots of places to eat on or nearby the square, so find someone you'd like to get to know better and head on out. Be back by one
thirty for our next critique session."

    After the talk, Avery found me in the back.

    "Hey! I'm so glad you're here. Want to grab some lunch?"

    "Sure, but Julia and I are old friends, so would it be okay if she
joins us?"

    Avery shrugged. "I guess so, sure."

    Julia approached and we hugged.

    "So, do you know Avery?" she asked.

    "Yes, we met at an event at the library here a few months ago.
We're about to go to lunch. Want to go with us?"

    "I'd love to."

    "I feel a bit out of my league here," Avery said. "A newbie

fantasy writer, a novelist, and a published university poetry professor?"

"But then there's your love of poetry, right? That's unusual for someone writing in your genre."

"Guess it is. Sure, let's go have some lunch. Where would you like to eat?"

"The square is going to be crowded and most of the restaurants there are pretty noisy, so why don't we go somewhere a little less known to the tourists? How about the University Club?" Julia offered.

"Are you a member?" I asked.

"Yep. I use it to entertain visiting faculty sometimes. Let's take my car."

We parked behind the club and walked upstairs for lunch. As Julia had suggested, it wasn't crowded, and we found a table by a window.

"Welcome back, Miss Wilson," a waitress said, handing us each a menu and a glass of water. "What would y'all like for lunch?"

I ordered first: "The chicken salad plate sounds good," I said, "and sweet tea."

"Same for me," said Julia.

"I'll have the meatloaf, mashed potatoes, and green beans, please. Oh, and unsweetened tea," Avery said.

After we got our drinks, Julia sipped her tea and started the conversation. "So, Avery, your writing is lyrical, and you love poetry, but I think there's something more at work here than your writing. How do you feel about telling us about your childhood?"

Avery and I exchanged looks, and then he repeated much of the same story he had told me on the balcony at Square Books earlier in the spring—about his adoptive family, his parents' birth son, and how he didn't fit in. He also talked about his ADD and subsequent drug use, and not finishing college.

"Full disclosure, Julia," I interrupted, "but Avery and I talked about some of this when I was here for the library event."

"Oh, I hope it doesn't feel like we're ganging up on you, Avery," said Julia.

"Well, I was a bit nervous coming to lunch with the two of you, but I really appreciate what you're trying to do. The workshop critique session was hard, emotionally, but I think it also cracked open my shell a bit."

"So, are you writing your fantasy novel as a way to create another universe, a different reality, than the one you grew up in?" Julia asked.

"I think so. I mean, a dystopian world can sound a little extreme, but you never know how quickly that other reality might become a present one."

Our food arrived and we ate quietly for a few minutes before Julia asked another question. "Have you ever wanted to search for your birth mother?"

Avery was caught a bit off guard but recovered himself as he swallowed another bite of meatloaf. "Yes, actually. But I haven't done anything about it yet. That's just like me, not to follow through with something, just like with my education."

"Why do you think you haven't searched for her yet?"

"Honestly, I think I'm afraid that if I found her, she wouldn't want me. It would be a worst rejection than the loneliness I feel with my adoptive family."

"But if you're not happy now, don't you think it would be worth the risk?" I asked.

"Maybe so." Looking at Julia he asked, "What about you? Do

you have kids?"

"No. I actually never married."

"Wow. That's a surprise. I mean, you're attractive and smart and creative. Oh, I guess that sounds kind of demeaning, like you're not good enough if you're not a wife or mother. I didn't mean it like that. I was just—"

"It's okay." Julia reached across the table and touched Avery's hand. Their eyes met, and I felt a kindness pass between them. Julia continued, "I get that all the time, and I know you weren't being mean. I had some bad experiences with men, really with boys, when I was young, and I guess I just closed that door and poured myself into my career. I write my feelings into my poetry and pour my motherly instincts into my students."

"I can see that you're good at both of those things." Avery smiled and relaxed, maybe for the first time all day.

"Oops! Time to get you back to the workshop. I'll get the check."

"Oh, no, I can buy my own lunch."

"Not at the University Club, you can't. Only members."

Julia signed the check and we headed back to her car. The drive back to the Depot was mostly quiet, and when she pulled up into the parking lot, Avery said, "Aren't you two coming in?"

"No, my part is done. I was just here to give a craft talk," said Julia.

"And I've got some work to do on a manuscript, so I'm headed to my hotel room. But I'll see you tomorrow for my craft talk."

He wore his disappointment on his face. "Oh, okay. Well, thanks so much for the lunch, Julia. Hey, since I live in town, maybe we can have coffee sometime. And I was also wondering if maybe I could audit one of your poetry classes."

       "Yes, to both of those! Now get back to the workshop and learn things!"

The afternoon critique sessions proved to be as emotion-packed as Avery's. Shannon, a girl who had been sexually molested by her grandfather, brought a chapter of her memoir in progress to the workshop. The other participants were kind in their criticisms of her writing, as was Grant, but the very act of sharing such personal events with a roomful of people had a similar effect on Shannon as Avery's simple confession that he was adopted.

       An older man had turned in a chapter of his World War II novel, which focused on a veteran with post-traumatic stress disorder. The message was powerful, but the prose needed work, and the advice the writer received could mean the difference between another manuscript that got stuck in a drawer forever and a powerful novel that made its way onto the shelves of bookstores and libraries for future readers. Avery wasn't sure what he had expected from the workshop—sweet little stories about Southern romance and Great-Aunt Bess's apple pie?—but the emerging writers who brought their stories with them left with the tools they needed to turn their rough drafts into polished manuscripts.

       When I walked into the Depot the next morning, I was glad to find Avery sharing some more relaxed chatter with his fellow students over coffee and doughnuts.

       "Hi, Adele." We shared a hug, and he introduced me to one of his new friends. Grant opened the session with a few housekeeping notes, and it was my turn. My craft talk was on using scenes and active verbs to strengthen prose. The students did a few exercises and the hour was over quickly.

       After another quick coffee break a panel formed in the front of the room. Everyone found their seats as the speakers from the weekend gathered for a final session, during which we would talk about the business end of writing—working with editors, literary agents, and publishers. One of the panel members was on faculty in the creative writing program at Ole Miss, like Julia was. One was a publicist. I took the third seat, and the fourth chair was empty. Five minutes after the panel was to begin, Grant addressed the room.

"Good morning. I hope everyone had fun at Taylor Grocery last night."

Smiles and murmurs filled the room.

"So, this morning we wanted to give y'all an opportunity to learn a bit about what to do with your manuscript once you've polished it, using some of the tools you gained during the workshop this weekend. I've invited the faculty who gave craft talks back to share their wisdom on this, and I apologize because Julia Wilson hasn't arrived yet. We'll go ahead and get started, and I'll try to reach her on her cell phone."

For the next hour, we talked about how to work with freelance editors to get the manuscript ready for its next step. We shared about the different paths to publishing, including the traditional paths of querying literary agents or independent presses, and the most recent trend of self-publishing.

I noticed Avery watch Grant leave the room during part of the session. We saw him through the window talking on his cell, and I wondered if something had happened to Julia. When the session was over and everyone was saying their goodbyes, we approached Grant.

"She's fine," Grant said. "Just something about a deadline she was chasing with her agent on her next book. It's really not like her to back out on a commitment, but I'm sure it was unavoidable."

Avery and I said goodbye to Grant and walked to my car.

"Are you going back to Memphis now?" he asked.

"Yeah, I need to get home."

He leaned against my car, hung his head, and moved the toe of his shoe across the gravel.

"Hey, are you okay? You opened up some old wounds in your conversation with Julia and me yesterday."

He nodded. "Yeah, I've definitely got a lot to think about. Thanks so much for spending time with me. Be safe driving home, and let's stay in touch."

We hugged and I took off.

Avery headed home, taking a different route to drive past Square Books and look up at the balcony where he and I had visited the day I spoke at the library. And then as he made his way around the roundabout and headed south down Lamar, he passed the University Club and thought about the things the three of us had talked about during our lunch. *Was that just yesterday?* He wished Julia had been on the panel at their morning session, and wondered if it would be weird of him to call her up just to talk sometime. He wasn't attracted to her romantically—and of course she was probably fifteen or twenty years older than him—but something about her drew him in.

Back to work at the library the next day, Avery thought about my visit in the spring, the day I talked at the Books and Lunch event. It was an easy reach to imagine himself doing that one day—speaking to a group of people about *his* book. But first he had to finish writing it. That was why he was only working part time, after all.

But the following days and weeks were difficult. He couldn't seem to keep his mind on the work. Every time he sat down to write— and immersed himself in the fantasy world he was creating on the page—his feelings about his birth mother grew stronger. The closer Balock and Ember got in their search for their birth parents in the book, the stronger his own desires grew. He remembered my words at lunch that day up at the University Club and wondered if I was right. Maybe it would be worth the risk.

Avery had been adopted through the Mississippi Children's Home in Jackson. He had looked them up online several years ago but never followed through. Their website didn't offer a link to search for birth parents, but it did have a phone number. His palms were sweaty as he punched the number into his cell.

"Mississippi Children's Home, this is Brenda."

"Um, yes, hello. My name is Avery Carmichael. I was adopted in 1992, and I was wondering how to initiate a search for my birth mother."

"Okay. I can help you with that, Mr. Carmichael. I assume you are calling because your adoptive parents used our placement services?"

"That's what they told me. So, is there some form I fill out, or what?"

"There are a couple of ways you can proceed. Of course, you are welcome to visit us in person if you'd like. Or there's an online form you can use."

"Are all the records open, or what?"

"No, actually some of the birth mothers haven't given their permission. But many have. How would you like to proceed?"

"Is there a fee?"

"Yes, one hundred twenty-five dollars, mostly to cover paperwork. You can pay by check or credit card, in person or online."

"How long does the search take?"

"Well, that depends. If your birth mother has also initiated a search, it could happen quickly. If not, you'll be looking at a longer search."

"Wow. This is surreal. I guess I'll do the online search. What's the link?"

The woman gave Avery the link to follow, and he filled out the form, including his credit card information, and was about to click SEND when a wave of nausea hit—the same old clouds of self-recrimination. *What if she doesn't want to meet me? What if we don't connect?* He took a deep breath and pushed the SEND key. It felt scarier than having the people at the workshop read and critique his writing. He felt exposed. *Too late now.* He would get back to work on the novel and try not to think about it.

Like that was going to happen.

Days went by. Finally, the woman at the adoption agency called him just as he was leaving for work at the library one morning.

"Avery? We've been processing your inquiry, and I'm afraid I have some bad news for you. We found a match for your date, but the birth mother has marked the records as closed. We aren't allowed to share them."

Avery's heart sank. As anxious as he was about the possibility of finally meeting his birth mother, having that option taken away was like a door slamming in his face.

"Isn't there anything I can do?"

"Some people have had success with lawsuits, but even if you do find her that way, she might not be receptive. Since she doesn't have the file marked open, she apparently hasn't started a search from her end. You might be setting yourself up for more pain. But of course that's completely up to you."

Brokenhearted and confused, Avery's first impulse was to speak with Julia, but he was actually kind of mad at her. But he also felt that she really cared about what happened to him—until she didn't show up for the Sunday morning panel at the workshop. *What was that about?*

He found her business card in his backpack and stared at her cell phone number. *Call or text?* A text would be safer, in case she didn't want to talk to him.

Hi. Julia. It's me, Avery, from the workshop. Can you chat?

He waited a few minutes. No reply. But as he put his phone in his pocket, he felt it vibrate.

Hello Avery. Sure. What's up?

He took a deep breath before typing his reply.

Can you meet me for a cup of coffee? I've got some difficult news and could really use someone to talk to.

Oh, sure. I've got a break after my class tomorrow morning. Meet you at Uptown Coffee around 10:30?

That would be great. Thanks. See you then.

Avery worked extra hours at the library that day. When his boss asked why he was still there two hours after his shift, he said he had been wanting to reorganize the children's section since the children's librarian had been out sick for a few days. Not really a lie, since he loved children's books and wanted their space to be welcoming. Some of his fondest childhood memories involved hours spent poring through library books while his brother was out playing ball.

After a restless night, it was finally the next morning. He arrived a few minutes early and ordered the house brand, black, and found a seat in the corner, where they would have a little more privacy. Julia walked in and waved at him from the front door before ordering a cappuccino, which she brought with her to the table.

"Good morning. It's so good to see you again, Avery," she said warmly.

"Hi. Thanks for meeting me. I wasn't sure if you would."

"Why not?"

"Because you didn't show up the last day of the workshop, and Grant couldn't really explain why. I wanted to call you that day, but I didn't want to intrude."

"I see. I think I told Grant that I was late on a deadline for a manuscript that was due to my agent, or something like that."

"Yeah, that's what he said. But is that really true?"

"Wow. You get right to it, don't you?" Julia shifted in her chair and sipped her cappuccino nervously.

"I'm sorry. I guess it's none of my business. Or maybe I'm trying to deflect my concerns onto you, since I've got something difficult to talk to you about."

Julia looked relieved and eager to shift the focus onto Avery. "Sure. Is something wrong?"

"Yeah, you could say that. Remember when we had lunch that day and Adele encouraged me to search for my birth mother?"

Julia nodded.

"Well, I did. And the agency where my parents adopted me said they couldn't give me any information about her, because she had marked the files as closed. When I asked what that meant, they said it meant she didn't want to found, basically. They said that birth mothers who want to be found usually initiate a search from their end, and she hadn't done that."

Julia took a deep breath, uncrossed her legs, and leaned her elbows on the table, resting her forehead on her clasped hands. Finally, she looked up and their eyes met.

"When were you born?"

"What? Oh, in 1992."

"Okay. What day?"

"June 30."

"And where were you born?"

"My adoption records list the University Hospital in Jackson, so I guess that's where. Why are you asking all these questions?"

Julia sat back in her chair and looked out the window. It was a pretty day, but there weren't many people in the chairs on the patio.

"Okay with you if we go outside? Where it's more private?"

Avery shrugged. "Sure, let's go."

They found a table in the shade along the outside wall of the building.

"So, that day I didn't show up for the workshop panel, I didn't have a deadline on a manuscript. I just didn't want to see you again."

"Why? Did I do something to upset you?"

"No, of course not. It's just that—well, I didn't know what was going on then, but now I'm pretty sure." She took a deep breath and wiped her eyes with a napkin from the table. "Here's the thing, Avery. When I was fifteen, I had a huge crush on a senior at my high school. He was tall, handsome, and real smart—editor of the school newspaper. And he was going away to college the next year. I was just a freshman, but I was working on the newspaper staff, writing feature stories, selling advertising, anything they'd let me do.

"Well, one afternoon we were working in the journalism room after school and he asked me out. I was floored. He usually only dated girls his age. That weekend I went with him to a football game, and afterwards I lost my virginity to him in the back seat of his car. It was September 30. The beginning of the school year, and I wondered what this might mean for us. Would he keep dating me, or was he just using me?"

Avery shifted in his chair, tossed his hair back, giving Julia a better view of his light-brown eyes, and folded his hands in his lap. He never took his eyes off Julia. "So, why are you telling me this?"

Julia stood and turned away from Avery, facing the opening at the back of the patio. Taking a deep breath, she turned back around. She was crying and could barely speak through her tears. "Because nine months later I had a baby. On June 30, 1992, at University Hospital in Jackson. I was sixteen and unmarried, so I gave . . . the baby up for adoption."

Avery jumped up from his chair, putting him face-to-face with Julia. He matched her tears with a flood of his own. He wanted to jump over the table and give her a big hug, but caution froze him.

"So, does this mean what I think it means? Are you saying that you could be my birth mother?"

"Yes. I mean, I think there are too many coincidences here. But we'll know for sure once I call the children's home and change the file status from closed to open."

"Do you want to do that? I mean, what do you want all of this to mean?"

"I want to call them right away, before we both get our hopes up too much."

"Our hopes? Does that mean you've changed your mind?"

"Yes! Before I met you, the baby—my son—was just an abstract being. And one I thought I could forget about one day. But the guilt never went away. And the shame for what happened when I was fifteen. But now, I'm looking at an amazing young man who just might have my DNA, and I couldn't be more hopeful."

They shared another hug and a rush of more tears. A few more customers found their way from the coffee shop out to the patio, but Julia and Avery didn't care about privacy anymore. They were both eager for the next chapter of their lives to begin, and they headed to Julia's house to make that phone call.

Sitting in her den with Avery, as awkward as two teenagers on a first date, Julia called the children's home. Avery could only hear her end of the call.

"Yes, this is Julia Wilson. I'm in your database as a birth mother from 1992. My files have been closed since then, but I'd like to change that now. What? Can't I just do it over the phone? Oh, I understand. Email the form and I'll get it notarized and send it back today. Why today? I've met a young man I believe might be my birth son. He inquired with you recently. His name is Avery Carmichael. Date of birth June 30, 1992. We're anxious to know if our files match. He's here with me now. Okay, thank you."

She looked at Avery and took a deep breath. "I guess you got the gist of that. I've got to download this legal form and sign it and get it notarized before she can open my file and tell us what we want to know."

Avery was pacing the room. "Can I come with you?"

"What about your job?"

"I'm off today. And besides, this is more important!"

Julia printed off the form, and they were out the door and off to a mail center to get it notarized. Back home less than an hour later, she scanned the form and emailed it back to the children's home. A few minutes later her cell rang.

"Yes? You got the form? Good. What's next?" Julia and Avery were sitting at a table in her study, near her computer and printer. Suddenly Julia jumped up and screamed, "Yes! Thank you so much! He's here with me now! I'll tell him."

Avery waited to hear the words.

"It's confirmed. You're my son! They want you to contact them to officially close out your search for your birth mother."

Avery stood quietly holding his mother in his arms. He still had so many questions—especially about his biological father—but they could wait. For now, he was anxious to nurture this new relationship. And to get back to his book, where Balock and Ember were still searching for their parents. It was pretty obvious where that story would end.

Back home in Memphis, I was thrilled to get a phone call from Avery, telling me the news of his discovery and his growing relationship with his birth mother. But then we lost touch for a year or two. And then one day I was searching the internet for literary events and came across a notice on Square Books' calendar for a reading and signing coming up the next month. Avery Carmichael would be reading from his debut dystopian fantasy novel, *The Orphan Rebellion*. I marked the date on my calendar. This was one literary event I wasn't going to miss!

Parenthood Redux

Jesus, Others, Yourself was the first thing that popped into my head when I read the theme for an upcoming issue of *Creative Nonfiction Journal* was JOY. I am sixty-five years old but that acronym from my Sunday School days back in the 1950s has somehow stuck with me. The way to be joyful, we were taught, was to love Jesus and others above ourselves, even though for decades since then, I have heard psychologists tout the importance of loving self. My subsequent spiritual journey has included many detours over bumpy roads, often knocking Jesus off the top tier of the love pyramid, but no matter his position in the equation, it is always *love of my children* that brings me the greatest joy.

At 9:45 on September 15, 1977, seven long years into our marriage the phone call finally came. "Mrs. Cushman? This is Mississippi Children's Home Society. We have a little boy who would like to meet you." That little boy was Jonathan, who was seventeen days old. When we arrived at the Children's Home the next day he was dressed in a white gown, sleeping in an antique wooden basinet lined with white lace linens. I thought my heart would burst as I held him in my arms, smiling through my tears at my husband Bill as he stood with his arms around both of us. It was a brand new feeling. At last, I knew *JOY!* Not just happiness—which comes and goes quickly with our changing circumstances—but something stronger. Something that felt at once earned and yet like the greatest gift I had ever received.

When I was sixteen I learned that I would not be able to biologically have children. At that age I wasn't too concerned about not being able to conceive. I worried about something darker. I was worried that I might have cancer or another such malady. So, when the doctor visited my hospital room after the exploratory surgery that summer of 1967, her news didn't undo me. I wasn't sick. I wasn't going to die. These are the things that plague the mind of a typical sixteen-year-old girl. It wasn't until a year later when I met the love of my life that the grief would set in.

At seventeen I fell in love with the man I would marry just two years later. I'll never forget Bill's reaction when I told him I couldn't have children. "We'll just adopt them!" And we did. But it wasn't as simple as it sounds. It never is. There was gnashing of teeth and many tears as I wept for my barren womb. I cried out to God for mercy. His answer came, but not with a physical miracle. Not with rejuvenated ovaries. But with words that helped me believe in a future with that could include joy. With these words from Psalm 30:

> O Lord my God, I cried to you for help, and you have
> healed me.
> Weeping may tarry for the night, but joy comes with the
> morning.

I remember all the times our best friends had babies. We would hurry to see them in the hospital, taking flowers or balloons and smiling and celebrating with each of them. And then I would cry my eyes out on the ride home. My grief would have been unbearable were it not for my aunt Barbara Jo.

Barbara Jo was my father's younger sister. She was only ten years older than I, and she always felt more like an older sister than an aunt. She had faced the same heartache of infertility when she was engaged to be married in the early 1960s. She understood my broken heart more than anyone and was always a great comfort to me. Not to mention the fact that I had two adopted first cousins—the son and daughter she and her husband adopted. My fondest holiday memories are of Thanksgivings at their house, where her nest was full and my heart was hopeful.

I said the gift of adoption felt *earned* because of how long and difficult the wait for our first child had been. The application process itself was daunting. We each were required to write autobiographies, including statements explaining why we wanted to adopt a child. A social worker visited our home to be sure we had a separate room for the baby, and that the environment was clean and safe. I was so nervous—it was like applying for a job, but with greater consequences. And there were times when I resented this intrusive, demeaning interrogation, which is what it felt like. Biological parents never have to go through such scrutiny.

And then came the *waiting*. When we first tried to apply at the adoption agency in 1970, we were only nineteen and twenty-one years old. Newlyweds. The social worker explained that they required at least a two-year marriage before a couple could make an application, and in our case—since my husband had just started medical school—they would prefer to wait until he finished school and had a stable income. This was their answer again, when we made our official application two years later. By then most of our friends in medical school had already started their families. Sure, many of us were living on borrowed money but our futures looked bright, didn't they?

After four years of waiting, the day came when Bill graduated and became a doctor. I called the agency to share the news and to remind them that we were certainly ready to be parents. They didn't seem to see it that way. We ended up waiting another three years—seven altogether—until Bill finished residency and started working full time at the Veterans Hospital in Jackson, Mississippi. Two months later the phone call finally came. After a seven-year wait, we now had twenty-four hours to prepare for our baby's homecoming.

I had actually decorated a nursery three years earlier—thinking we would be allowed to adopt at the end of medical school. But when we moved to a different house during residency, I couldn't bring myself to set the crib up again, or hang the pictures of animals and alphabets on the walls of our guest room/potential nursery. The boxes of diapers, stuffed animals, toys, and other supplies would remain in the attic until the phone call came. Now, we were to pick up our son the next day. I don't know whether it was adrenaline, necessity (so much to get done!), or joy that fuelled my flurry of activities as I ran out shopping for formula, dragged all the baby items down from the attic and decorated another nursery—this time with the assurance that it would soon become a place of stories and songs and sleep and play and, yes, joy. I do remember that I didn't sleep that night.

Jonathan did come home with us the next day. Our lives changed forever.

My parents were out of town, so we surprised them by leaving a note on their door that said: "Jonathan David Cushman would like to meet his grandparents. Please come soon." Jonathan David means "beloved gift of the Lord." Papaw and Granny Effie arrived the next day with a bottle of Pouilly-Fuissé, which has remained a favorite French chardonnay of ours to this day, almost forty years later.

Jon was an affectionate baby, an easy toddler. Although I was jealous of my friends who were breast-feeding their babies, I quickly discovered the convenience of bottle feeding a baby who had been put on a schedule by the sweet women who worked in the nursery at the children's home where he spent the first seventeen days of his life. He only woke for one feeding during the night and went right back to sleep.

Within a few months he was sleeping through the night. Jon hit all the developmental milestones on or before target, growing into a handsome, smart, athletic little boy. It was time for a little brother.

We contacted Mississippi Children's Home Society just a year or two after adopting Jon, asking when we could apply for another baby. We wanted our son to know the joy of having siblings, and we wanted to increase our own joy as parents. The bad news was that the same people who had told us how important it was for adopted children to have brothers or sisters now told us that the waiting list had grown and it could be many years before another child was available to us. More waiting. Again we watched our friends' families grow, and we longed for an increase of children's voices in our own home.

Several years later I saw an article in our local newspaper about people who had adopted children from South Korea and other countries through an organization known as Holt International. This group was hosting an event for prospective adoptive parents. I eagerly shared the article with Bill and we knew immediately this is what we wanted to do. Taking Jon with us to the gathering, which was filled with families of a variety of races, including biological and adopted children from the U.S. and other countries, hearing their stories and seeing the joy in their lives, we asked where to sign up.

This time the wait was only nine months. It felt like a pregnancy of sorts! Jonathan was almost six when we applied, so we asked for a little brother, a toddler rather than a baby, which we believed would help in their bonding as brothers. Ahn, Soo Jin (the last name comes first in Korea) arrived in January of 1984 at age two years and eight months. We named him Jason Chandler—giving him a family name, Chandler, to go with his surname, Jason, which means "healer." He certainly brought lots of healing to our family over the years, and great joy! He was full of energy and laughter and sensitivity. It wasn't always easy for him, growing up in a white family in the South, going to school with whites and Blacks and only a few Asians. I guess the flipside to the joy was the pain of watching him experience teasing for being different. Would a Korean girl suffer the same in our Mississippi community? We were about to find out. All that was missing now was a daughter.

About a year later we applied with Holt again, and this time it only took four short months before Won, Me Ai arrived from South Korea, at age two years, eleven months. We named her Elizabeth Ann and called her Beth. She was incredibly beautiful (still is) but she took a few weeks to warm up to her new country, her new home, her new family. Unlike outgoing Jason, Beth held her feelings close to her heart, and blessed us immediately with her gifts of intuition, loyalty, and a peaceful kind of charm one usually only sees in older girls and young women. She would excel in everything she did—from academics to art to athletics—but she also experienced some incidents of prejudice as a teenager. More pangs to my heart, but always there was the joy.

All three of our adopted children are exceptional in many ways. Very smart, and of course they are all beautiful—our two Asians and our white son—all different, all wonderful. And yet all three have had to find their way in the world without their birth families. This is something I think most people rarely recognize as the huge wound it can be for children who are put up for adoption by their birth mothers, either as infants, toddlers or older children, sometimes spending time in orphanages along the way, as Jason and Beth both did. They each fulfilled my dreams to be a mother, but what about *their* dreams? What about *their* opportunities for joy?

Let's start with Jonathan. On August 30, 2017, Jon will be forty. He has lived an exceptional life—overcoming struggles that are unknowable to most of us and paramount for an adopted child. He served in the Army from 2001-2013, which included two tours in Iraq and one in Afghanistan. He became a helicopter pilot, and now, in his retirement from military service, he flies a med-evac helicopter—saving lives on a daily basis. He has followed his love of all things tasteful (he's a sommelier and gourmet cook) to New Orleans, where he now lives with his wife.

Jason is next. He's the one who visited his homeland of South Korea twice—once with a group at age eighteen, and again on his own at twenty-one—searching for his birth mother and sister. He overcame overwhelming grief at hearing that his birth mother would not meet with him. Nor could he learn where his birth sister now lived. He moved on with his life, marrying a wonderful Hmong woman in 2008. When their first child Grace was born in 2009, I flew to Denver to be there for this momentous event. He handed her to me with tears in his eyes, saying, "Look, Mom, now I have a birth family." More joy. This event was followed quickly by the birth of his second daughter, Anna Susan (yes, she is named for me!) in 2010, and his family continues to fill me with great joy. He and his wife See both work in IT in Arizona, own a lovely home, and are experiencing the joy of raising two terrific daughters.

Beth married a wonderful African American man—whom she had met during their college days at the University of Tennessee—in 2010, and surprised me by asking me to be Maid of Honor at her wedding. "But, don't you just want me to fill the traditional role of Mother of the Bride?" I asked. "You are my best friend," was her reply. I cannot tell you the joy I felt at those words. We held the wedding at my favorite place on earth—Seagrove Beach, Florida—at sunset on a beautiful May afternoon. She didn't wait long to share more joyful news. Her first child, Gabby, was born the following April. But here comes bigger joy—my presence was requested in the birthing room. And so I flew to Denver and rented a condo for five weeks and received another incredible gift as I participated with her and her husband in this miracle of birth, which I was never allowed to experience personally. Gabby and I have been joined at the hip since that day. A difficult birth but a wondrous outcome. I wondered if she would ever be brave enough to endure this again.

But she did. In August of 2015 she gave birth to Izzy, while I waited at her home with three-year-old Gabby. When Gabby and I arrived at the hospital the next day, I knew Beth's family was complete. Our joy was multiplied. Beth and her husband Kevin are also in IT in Denver, also homeowners, also experiencing the joy that many families may take for granted.

I'm not sure which joy is greater—the earlier delight of adopting these children, or the later ecstasy of seeing them flower as young adults and eventually watching two of them experience the establishment of their own birth families. Jesus has definitely been with us during this journey, and will always be the first letter (J in JOY) of this amazing experience for me.

The Other Woman
2008

From the beginning I wondered if he might go back to her. He hadn't seen her in almost twenty years. One day, in the summer of 2000, he came home from an overseas trip with a photograph of her and put it in a little frame. We even talked about her from time to time. I always thought I was open-minded about these things. And then a woman who lives half way around the world shattered my faith in the golden calf of motherly love with the hard edge of her own broken humanity.

It all started in 2002, during the Christmas holidays. Our two adopted Korean children—Jason and Beth—were both home from the University of Tennessee. Beth and I were baking Christmas cookies when Jason came into the kitchen and sat down at the table.

"Mom, I need to talk to you about something."

I put the last dirty cookie sheet into the sink, wiped my hands on the green and red plaid dish cloth and poured another cup of coffee.

"OK, what's up?"

"Well, you know I've been messing up at school again this semester." He cleared his throat and continued. "I just don't ... seem to care much any more." The smell of real butter and sugar and cinnamon filled the air. The happy faces of snowmen and angels adorned the racks of sugar cookies that covered the kitchen counters. Christmas music intruded on our conversation from a commercial on the television in the den.

He hung his head, and then stared out the window. Jason had been on academic probation more than once, due to his inability to focus on his studies. After a medical reaction to Adderall, he hadn't been on any meds for his Attention Deficit Disorder in several months.

I took another sip of coffee and nibbled at a plate of sugar cookie fragments, broken pieces that didn't make it to the decorating platters. "So, what do you think might help?"

"Well, I was wondering if I could use my second-semester college funds for another trip to South Korea."

Jason had been to the land of his birth the summer after he graduated from high school. A group of adoptees between the ages of 18 and 30 traveled together from the US to various cities in Korea. Some of them had filed legal paperwork ahead of time, which started the official search for their birth mothers. Most of them visited the orphanages where they had lived before they were adopted by American families. The trip had actually been my idea. As sweet as my little Korean son had always been, he never felt at home in our Western culture. And he always seemed to have a yearning for something we couldn't give him.

During the tour, they had met with a group of young, unwed pregnant girls at one of the agency's facilities. The idea was for the girls to tell their stories, and to ask the adoptees how they felt about being adopted—kind of a two-way exchange of information and emotion. When Jason called home to tell us about the experience, I could hear his tears and feel his grief begin to surface.

"I wish I had done the paperwork to start a search for my birth mom while I'm here. Being with these girls really makes me want to meet her now."

"Maybe you can start the process when you get home."

"Yeah, but I leave for college in a few weeks. I don't know how that's gonna' work."

Jason entered the University of Tennessee that fall, and immediately sought out a circle of Asian friends. He immersed himself in Asian culture, as much as he could in Eastern Tennessee, cooking Korean meals and dating Asian girls. Trying to concentrate on school while his heart was in Korea didn't work so well. Self-medicating with alcohol and pot for his ADD and his grief didn't help the situation. He began spiraling downwards.

Two and a half years later, he was frustrated by his long-distance efforts to find his birth mother, even with all the tools the Internet has to offer.

"How do you think going back to Korea might help?" I ventured, offering Jason a Christmas cookie from one of the racks cooling near the stove. Sugar and butter—southern comfort foods. He acknowledged the gesture but left the cookie alone on the napkin in front of him. It was an angel cookie.

"The social worker in Korea is such a jerk. He just gives me the runaround. I think the only way I might possibly find her is to go there myself."

"OK. So, how will you go about the search, once you get there?"

"Rob's mother is gonna' help me." Jason's roommate in Knoxville was half Korean.

"She's going to Seoul to visit relatives this summer. I know it sounds crazy, but I really need to go."

"I'll talk with your father about it." The words hung heavy in the air, but my hug reassured Jason that his dad would cooperate.

The following July, Rob's mother actually located Jason's birth mom while Jason was in Korea, but she refused to see him. He had been looking for her for three years, had traveled seven thousand miles to meet her, and she said no. She not only wouldn't *meet* him, she wouldn't even *speak* with him.

My initial response was colored by memories of something that happened almost 30 years ago. We had just adopted Jonathan, our old-est son. It was a domestic adoption, but it took seven years from the time we applied to the day we brought Jon home from the Mississippi Children's Home Society. He was two weeks old.

I sat, holding him in my arms, watching a television documen-tary about the emotional struggle that unwed mothers go through when they give their babies up for adoption. I remember feeling like a traitor. Like I was the bad guy—the one who had taken someone's baby away from them. I cried as I held this precious child in my arms and watched images of teenage girls weeping for the children they had lost. My ra-tional mind told me they were only children themselves, not ready to be mothers. But still, as I held another woman's child in my arms and called him Jonathan David—Beloved Gift of the Lord—I felt respon-sible for her pain.

So, when my second adopted son was plunged into the dark pit of grief and depression by his birth mother's rejection, I didn't weep for her. I was angry. Yes, of course I understood that the culture in South Korea isn't kind to unwed mothers. I knew she might have extenuating circumstances. And I couldn't imagine the pain it might cause her to be reminded of what she gave up, if she met her precious son face to face or held him in her arms, now, at age 21. But I also believed that the pain was hers to own.

We adopted Jason when he was almost three. We changed his legal name from Ahn Soo Jin to Jason Chandler Cushman. Jason means healer. Chandler is a family name on my husband's side. He was a bun-dle of joy as a toddler, eagerly embracing his new world and his new family. When we adopted our three-year-old Korean daughter nearly two years later, he welcomed her with brotherly love and a protective spirit that endures even now.

Over the years, friends have asked how I would feel if any of my children ever wanted to find their birth mother. Would I feel hurt? Jealous? Would I see their desire as a personal rejection? If it had happened when Jason was younger, maybe I would have felt threatened. But Jason always made it clear that he loved us. "You and Dad are the best thing that ever happened to me," he had said, more than once. This wasn't about *us*. It was about *her*. The other woman.

Her name is Kim, Ei Soo. Jason had it painted in calligraphy on a colorful wall hanging he bought on his first trip to Korea. Along with his biological sister's name, Ahn, Jong Hee. The banner hung in his room for a long time, a vivid expression of his longing and devotion.

The orphanage in Korea had given him a photo of his sister when she was about five years old, which he framed and kept by his bed. She is three years older than him.

"They told me she might have also been adopted by someone in the States," he explained when he showed me the picture. "But they said they don't have any record of who or where." That was back in 2000.

"Did Rob's mother ask about your sister when she spoke with your birth mother?" I asked when Jason called from Seoul with the news in July of 2003.

"Yeah," his voice cracked. "She's living with our mother here in Korea, but she won't let me see her or talk with her, either."

I couldn't find any words that could help Jason make sense of this painful rejection. I thought about saying, "Oh, Jason, you know this isn't about *you*. I'm sure she loves you and has issues we know nothing about." But, how could he possibly depersonalize her actions? He is her *son*. So I just wept with him.

Jason's struggles to close this chapter of his life are never ending. It's been almost five years since that disappointing trip to Korea, and I can't help but wonder if he looked for his birth mother in the Asian girls he dated during that time. He recently married a lovely young Hmong woman. She has her own stories to grieve, as her people fled their country after the Vietnam War. Her parents lived in a refugee camp in Thailand for several years before coming to the States in the '70s.

The healing process for Jason is slow. As it is for me. I love all three of my children. They were each given to me by women who couldn't take care of them for various reasons. Over the years I have prayed for each of them. For their peace concerning the decisions they made. For God to comfort them. I have tried to see things through their eyes, and to love them.

But now I can only see the pain my own children have suffered. I recently became part of an adoptive mothers support group. The group of 11 mothers has 17 adopted children altogether, ranging in age from 5 to 31. Our children were adopted from five different countries, counting the U.S. Mine are the oldest in the group. We've been learning about how important the grief process is—for us, as adoptive mothers, to grieve our loss of not being able to bear these children in our wombs. And the grief our adopted children need to acknowledge, for the mother whose voice they heard for nine months while they were in her womb. The loss of family, of roots, and sometimes even of an entire country and culture.

Helping children from another country bond with their adoptive parents and acclimate to their new world has its own set of challenges. It's hard to feel them pull away so quickly when I try to hug them. Harder, still, to watch them struggle with—or repress—their pain. Difficult to celebrate their birthdays every year without remembering their abandonment. It takes courage to help them enter into their search for love and identity without the benefit of roots—of connectedness.

But who would have thought that the hardest part would be learning to forgive the other woman.

myPod
2007

My daughter came home from grad school with the ultimate Father's Day gift for her dad—an iPod Nano. To be more specific, a light metallic blue iPod Nano. As she began to show him how to download the music from his (evidently out-of-date) Mp3 Player, she looked at him and said, "Okay, Dad, what do you want to name it?"

"Name *what?*"

"Your iPod."

"Oh—I didn't know it needed a name."

"How 'bout 'Baby Blues'?" I jumped in from my nearby perch on the couch.

"That works," my daughter began to enter the name into the tiny sliver of metal.

"Why 'Baby Blues'?" my husband asked.

"Because your gadget-thingy is the color of your eyes and it's tiny like a baby and it plays music and we live in Memphis, home of the blues."

It took a minute for it to sink in, and then my husband asked, "So, what would you name *your* iPod Nano if you had one?"

I was quick with my answer, "peapod."

"peapod?" Father and daughter asked in unison.

"Yes. I want one in pea green. You know, the color of new life that germinates from the seeds inside the pod and grows into a verdant garden of music."

My husband looked at our daughter and said, "Your mother has been writing poetry again."

He was right. And you know, one purpose of poetry is the *naming* of things. Throughout history poets have understood the necessity of giving names to things and events so we won't forget their significance—their meaning. It started in the Garden, when God named Adam and Eve. Then he told Adam to name the animals. How cool would that be? Imagine, for example, looking at a brown furry football-shaped animal which was covered in long sharp needles that could shoot out of its body and saying, "Hmmmm—*porcupine.*"

Parents take great care (or they *should*) in naming their children, sometimes passing on a family name with all its baggage and expectations. Others seek to imbue their offspring with help from on high, naming them after saints or angels or even the Holy Mother Mary herself. In the Eastern Orthodox Christian tradition, Godparents sometimes do the naming, on the eighth day after the child's birth. There is even a ceremony for it. Name Days (feast days of patron saints) are often celebrated with more pomp than birthdays.

Children know the importance of names. How many times has a child run inside crying to his mother, "He called me a *name!*"? And sometimes those names stick like duct tape throughout childhood and adolescence and even into adulthood, branding someone forever as a "crybaby" or "fatso" or worse.

Remember the Johnny Cash song, "A Boy Named Sue"? It tells a poignant story about the power of a name. The father gives his son a sissy girl-name to teach him to be tough, knowing that Sue will have to fight his way through all the teasing brought on by his name. Of course, in the end the son says that when *he* has a boy he'll name him Bill or George or *anything but Sue.*

Companies often hire creative people to give names to their products, building their image and increasing sales. You might think you're above their tactics, but consider this: would as many women buy Spanx if they were called "Support Tights" or "Middle Shapers"? And how many of us girls are immune to the affect of nail polish pigment names like "Smokin' in Havana," "Bubble Bath" and "Root Beer Float"?

What did you think the first time you picked up a copy of *skirt!* Magazine… that it was going to address *women's* issues, right? Big deal—lots of magazines do that. But didn't something about the way the name was written make you think it might take a fresh view of things? I was hooked right away by the lower case "s' and the forward-slanting *"i"* with its hair blowing in the breeze. I immediately thought, *this is going to be dynamic, with a powerful feminine kick.* The exclamation point at the end shouts "excitement!" All that in five letters and a punctuation mark. Never underestimate the power of a name.

If you still aren't convinced that people pay attention to names, check out best-selling author Joshilyn Jackson's (*gods in Alabama; Between, Georgia*) August 15 post on her blog, "Faster Than Kudzu." Her family was getting a kitten. Her blog post was like a "call for names," and would you believe over sixty people wrote in with suggestions? Here's a sampling: Katmandu, Piggle, Catastrophic Bubba, Piewhacker, Neva Bean, Crack, Newt (for a neutered cat), Zoloft, and Prozac.

After two days of considering all the write-ins, she posted a picture of this precious, yellow and white kitten. The title of her blog post on August 17 was "Meet *Sanity* Jackson." Sanity. *Perfect*, I thought. But then she said Sanity wasn't really his name and that she's still considering her options, including Hooky-do, "because his hands are made out of Velcro." *Hooky-do?* Hey, but it's working. I'm checking her blog every day to find out what she names that kitten!

As a writer, I spend a lot of time naming things—books, book chapters, short stories, poems, even blogs. Mine is called "Pen and Palette." I went through about twenty five names before I came up this one. I wanted the name to accomplish at least three things: (1) Identify me as a writer; (2) identify me as an artist; and (3) make a subtle play on Flannery O'Connor's insistence that a writer must learn to "paint with words."

Again and why bother? Because a name is the first, and sometimes last, opportunity the writer has to hook you, the reader. And because it's fun. And because naming is our God-given right, just like God told Adam in the Garden.

And so I ask you, would you have read this article if the title had been "The Importance of Names" or even "What's In a Name"? *Maybe.* But hopefully when you saw the name, "myPod," your curiosity was peaked and you made a decision to read on. To at least invest in the first paragraph. Now, here you are at the end, and I hope it was worth the read. If nothing else, whether or not you're a poet, maybe you'll give it a little more thought the next time you name something… even your iPod.

V

PLACE

Southern writers have a great sense of place. That makes you write the truth. When you do that, people read it and say, "You wrote my life."

—*Maggie Britton Vaughan (Poet Laureate of Tennessee)*

Every story would be another story, and unrecognizable if it took up its characters and plot and happened somewhere else.... Fiction depends for its life on place. Place is the crossroads of circumstance, the proving ground of What happened? Who's here? Who's coming?

—*Eudora Welty*

Are *These* My People?

A reluctant daughter of the Old South searches for her roots.

2009

"Let's drive down to the Neshoba County Fair!"

It was a hot day in July and I was with my friends in the Yoknapatawpha Writers Group that meets monthly in Oxford, Mississippi to critique each other's works-in-progress. The fair is an event I'd heard about my whole life, but had never attended. Part of the impetus was that Oxford author, Tom Franklin, would be reading from his story in the anthology, *Southern Fried Farce.* Tom would be part of the Thacker Mountain Radio Show, which usually broadcasts from Off Square Books in Oxford on Thursday nights.

When we arrived around 7:30 that night, cars were parked along both sides of Highway 21 for a mile in either direction of the front gate, in addition to filling up a huge cow pasture that had been set up for parking across the road. Once inside, the sub-culture that is the Neshoba County Fair nearly took my breath away.

First it was the cabins. Six hundred darling, I mean *darling,* little two-story cabins decorated in shabby chic colors and furnishings with strings of lights and Japanese lanterns everywhere. Some of these cabins have been in certain families for generations. My friend Doug told me that the ones around "Founder's Square," the pavilion that's used for political speeches and literary readings and musical entertainment, are worth a fortune. In Philadelphia, Mississippi? How can that be? But as I looked around, I saw generations of people who looked like old money—Mississippi beauty queens and golden boys.

My first reaction was, "I need a beer."

Doug laughed and said, "It's a dry county." And then, answering the shock on my face, he explained, "Oh, there's plenty of beer. You can bring in as much as you want to. You just can't sell it."

My throat suddenly constricted and my nerves got edgy as I watched people entertaining dozens of guests on their front porches around the square, all sipping wine and beer from plastic cups. Many of the folks looked like they could have been in my sorority or my husband's fraternity at Ole Miss in the seventies. So I thought surely I'd find someone I knew that I could go up to and say, "Hi! Remember me?" and then somehow work into, "I didn't know you couldn't buy drinks here," in my best Southern-eze.

But as I searched the crowd, while everyone looked familiar in a generic sort of way, there was no one I could put a name with. And I began to wonder: who *are* these people? Everywhere I looked I saw thin, gorgeous women and girls with beautiful hair and luminous faces, some in strapless sun dresses and sandals or cute little rain boots, others in shorts or capris or jeans with tank tops or peasant blouses. All sporting the quintessential Southern accessory—an even tan. And golden boys with khaki shorts or jeans and button-down-collar long-sleeved shirts rolled up to the elbows or t-shirts with sports logos on them. A few cowboy hats and boots and more than a few aging yuppies, but for the most part, they all seemed to be aging well.

Tom's reading was great. Afterwards, being the gracious person he is, he went to a cabin and came back to the square with two cups of cold beer, one for himself and one for me! We shared a few laughs, especially when Tom said he had considered, for a moment, up there on that stage where so many Southern politicians have given speeches over the years, raising his hand in the air at the end of his reading and shouting, "Obama '08!" We shook our heads—probably not a good idea in that setting. It was then, as we stood around and talked shop for a while with Tom that it hit me: Are *these* my people? Not the thousands of Beautiful People in the pavilion and the cabins, but the half-dozen struggling writers standing around our friend and mentor in a semi-circle. It was in that circle that I felt at home.

In the larger circle that is the Neshoba County Fair, a micro-cosm of the Old South, there was not one Black person to be found on that Saturday night. *Not one.* In a state that has the highest percentage of African Americans of any of the fifty, not one of them had come to Mississippi's Giant Houseparty®. I mentioned this to someone that night, and he said, "I've never thought about that. They could come if they wanted to, but I guess this just isn't their thing."

Not their thing? Great music and political speakers and literary readings and food and beer outside on a summer night in Mississippi? Black people wouldn't like that?

Or could it have something to do with the fact that less than three miles from the Neshoba County Fair, in 1964, three civil rights workers' bodies were found buried on Olen Burrage's Old Jolly Farm, having been savagely beaten and shot three times? The juxtaposition of that part of Mississippi's history with the fun and games of the Beautiful People on that summer night in July was a powerful but difficult image to hold in my head.

Driving home to Memphis, the image grew stronger. I was born in Jackson, Mississippi, in the segregated fifties and came of age in the apocalyptic sixties before moving to Memphis in 1988. I'm continuing to try to connect with my roots as I hone my craft with other writers down in Oxford. But as I think about the Beautiful People at the Neshoba County Fair, and the writers and artists and musicians who had been invited there to celebrate life together in Mississippi—*without* their beautiful Black neighbors—I still wonder, are *these* my people?

The Wind in the Trees
2013

Like so many visits to Oxford, Mississippi, our day began with coffee at High Pointe, shopping at the cute little boutiques on the square, and browsing the shelves at Square Books. My best friend from Little Rock was with me, and we had plans to meet up with some of our writing buddies and possibly take in a few flicks at the Oxford Film Festival. It was February 7, 2009.

Over lunch with author Jere Hoar *(Body Parts, The Hit)* at the Downtown Grill, the conversation returned to the topic Daphne had been pursuing during our drive down from Memphis—*the land.*

It might help you to know that Daphne was born on a ranch in Mexico, and her people inhabit various geographical areas across Texas and Arkansas. But like me—and a growing number of other lovers of Southern literature and the sense of place that nurtures it— she's nursing a post school-girl crush on the city of Oxford. And she didn't even attend the hallowed halls of the University of Mississippi as I did. As a coed during the turbulent sixties and perplexing seventies, I remember sitting in the Faulkner Library, writing a ridiculously fluffy paper on *The Sound and the Fury*, hoping to disguise my complete lack of understanding of Faulkner's brilliance with bullshit masquerading as higher criticism.

But on this particular Saturday, our excursion took us down a road never traveled by this Mississippi native. We were looking to buy some land near Oxford. Well, my friends were looking, and at this point I was just along for the ride. We had picked up a copy of *The Oxford Ea-gle* at Off Square Books after lunch, so Daphne could check out the real estate section while I drove. But it turned out that our friend Doug had a detour in mind that would lead us deeper inside a mystical world that lies just south of Oxford in the peaceful Yocona community. We were headed to Larry Brown's beautiful hidden paradise—the place where one of Oxford's favorite native sons created his special literary magic. Brown, known for his gritty fiction (*Big Bad Love*, *Joe*) and candid portrayal of life in the rural South, died in November of 2004, at the young age of 53. Doug had attended the funeral. This was his first return trip to Brown's property, and his mood was pensive.

"Turn right down that road," Doug said, as we continued south on a rural highway about ten minutes outside Oxford. The road twisted and turned, as fields and trees and an occasional barn or homestead appeared on either side.

"I think it's just around this next curve, on the left… look—the gate is down, you can pull in."

We pulled onto the property, got out of the car and stood silently, taking in the scene. To the left was an old barn, in just enough disrepair to tease an artist's brush or a photographer's lens. Straight ahead the dirt road, partly overgrown with grass, took us down a slight incline towards an idyllic setting—a sparkling pond, surrounded by massive trees. An old fishing boat was barely visible near the edge, camouflaged by tall grass. Tackle boxes and fishing rods leaned against a nearby tree.

"Listen," Daphne stopped our movement. "You can hear the wind in the trees."

I think it was the first time I had heard that sound since my last visit to a Monastery in Michigan, nearly two years ago. You can't hear the wind in the city, with all the competing noises. And this was a completely different sound than the wind at the beach, where water and sand serve as woofers and tweeters for the otherwise silent strength of the ocean breeze. The wind in the trees by Larry Brown's pond had a powerful upward pull on my senses, as I looked skyward, and then involuntarily closed my eyes and took in a deep breath.

We felt like we were walking on sacred ground as we continued our stroll deeper into the heart of the property.

"I need a moment," Doug's voice was quiet. We watched him ascend a low hill towards the barn, the site of two graves. Larry Brown and his wife had lost an infant daughter at one point. Her tiny tombstone mirrored his larger one, like a doe in the shadow of its stately parent.

Daphne and I found the dock on the pond, and Doug joined us later, sitting on the benches and taking in the reflection of the huge trees in the water.

"What's that tiny house on the other side of the pond?" I asked.

"Oh, that's The Shack," Doug's voice was gravelly. "That's where Larry did a lot of his writing."

Daphne and I walked around the pond to get a closer look, and what we found was enchanting. A one-room edifice, which still held relics of Brown's days and nights spent honing his craft within those four small walls. A simple couch. Partly burned candles. Photographs of his family. An old stereo. And an incredible view of the pond. There was a deck in front of the house—its footprint at least at large as the interior of the building—and from that deck the sound of the wind in the trees was amplified. The trees were massive, a reminder that the land had been here long before our generation arrived. That's when Daphne brought us back to thoughts of her quest.

"This would work. Yes, this would be perfect. Seven acres with a slight hill, a barn and a pond."

Of course Larry Brown's property wasn't for sale, but it set the bar for other candidates. On the drive back into Oxford, we continued to observe the expanses of open fields and meadows between the houses and trailers that dotted the landscape.

"You wouldn't want that piece," Doug would say, as our eyes scanned the terrain. "It's bottom land, and it floods when it rains." We noticed water standing in patches in some areas as he spoke. "But that one up there would give you a great view." Our eyes would follow his like hunters in the path of trained bird dogs. And we would sigh and mumble fragments of words or phrases that were inadequate reflections of our hearts' longings.

Back in town we met back up with our friends for drinks on the balcony at City Grocery, and later at the Lyric for the film festival awards show. Our friend and mentor, the poet, Beth Ann Fennelly, was one of the MCs, and she and her husband, Tom Franklin, also an author, were enjoying their daughter's acting debut. Both venues were noisy and fun, full of laughter and people celebrating life and art, usually just my cup of tea. But on this evening my party girl spirits were slightly subdued by memories of an afternoon this city girl wouldn't soon forget.

Even up on that balcony overlooking the square in downtown Oxford—one of my favorite haunts—I realized that something was missing. Something I had discovered out at Larry Brown's farm—the sound of the wind in the trees.

The Crossroads of Circumstance: Setting in Southern Literature
2010

One of the optional themes for this cycle of posts here at A Good Blog is "setting."

Setting: "The manner, position, or direction in which something is *set*." That's the first of three definitions of "setting," according to Webster. In fact, you have to read down to part b of the third definition to get to setting as it pertains to writing: "the time and place of the action of a literary, dramatic, or cinematic work."

But I think Webster had it right the first time, even from a literary standpoint. Why? Because the "setting"—the time and place of a story—does much to set the manner, position, or direction of the story.

And since this blog is about how southern authors spin their stories, I was curious to see what my fellow Jackson, Mississippi, native, Eudora Welty has to say about setting:

Every story would be another story, and unrecognizable if it took up its characters and plot and happened somewhere else.... Fiction depends for its life on place. Place is the crossroads of circumstance, the proving ground of What happened? Who's here? Who's coming?

I think this is true, but only in a broad sense, geographically. *To Kill a Mockingbird*, set in a small town in Alabama, would not have worked in another part of the country, but it could have worked in a small Mississippi town, don't you think? My friend, Tom Franklin, was banking on this when he did just that—he changed the setting of his *New York Times* best-seller, *Crooked Letter, Crooked Letter*, from a small town in Alabama to a town just over the state line in Mississippi. *Why?* According to Tom, it was in order to make the book fit the title he came up with. Most everyone recognizes "Crooked Letter, Crooked Letter" as part of the sing-song method of teaching children to spell Mississippi:

> *M i crooked letter crooked letter i crooked letter crooked letter i hump back hump back i*

Yes, he did that. A smart marketing move? Probably so. But knowing Tom, it was purely aesthetics. And it worked. (On October 15 it was number 24 on the *NYT* Best Sellers List.)

My favorite author is Pat Conroy. And though some folks say he's made his fortune with a cottage industry built on stories about his dysfunctional family, (and yes, I'm drawn to those stories) his literary genius is what keeps me coming back for more. And part of that genius is his use of setting.

"My wound is geography." These are the first four words in my favorite book of all time, Conroy's *The Prince of Tides*. And he does it again with the opening sentence in *South of Broad*: "It was my father who called the city the mansion on the river." This time he's writing about Charleston.

Conroy's stories probably could not have been set anywhere but in the low country that gives them their very life. For his stories, setting is a leading character—in the case of *South of Broad*, that character is the *city* of Charleston. His protagonist, Leo, says of Charleston, "I carry the delicate porcelain beauty of Charleston like the hinged shell of some soft-tissued mollusk."

Maybe it's risky for me to set my novel-in-progress in a state in which I've never lived (Georgia) rather than my home state of Mississippi, but like Tom Franklin, there's a method to my madness. My protagonist needs the small town rural environs of the northern part of the state of Georgia for her childhood as well as the Savannah College of Art and Design (SCAD) and the eclectic city of Savannah as the setting for certain stages of her story. And yes, she'll even make a visit to Conroy's beloved Charleston, but it won't be her wound. And that's all I'm going to say about that for now.

I've only addressed one aspect of setting so far—*place*. What about the other aspect that's often included in its definition—*time*? I'm not a scholar, but it seems that where place is integral to the characters and plot, time has more to do with technique. It's the author's choice to use chronological time, flashbacks, jumping around from chapter to chapter, or other techniques for dealing with time. In my work-in-progress, I'm playing with stream-of-consciousness—a la Faulkner, Woolf, and most recently, Michael Cunningham, in his work, *The Hours*. I love interior monologue as a vehicle for unpacking the complexity of human lives. I'm hoping to weave those monologues through the lives of three women from very different times and places, whose destinies intersect in a mystical way.

"Mary of Egypt"—the Opera
Excerpt from *Cherry Bomb*

Chapter Fourteen

As they entered the Wells Theatre on Saturday night, Mare and Elaine were greeted by materials, textures, and geometric angles that were part of its Art Moderne splendor. Intricate rectangular carvings repeated themselves along the walls. Gold leaf flickered off every surface. Even the curtain on the massive stage was itself a work of art—tapestries of shimmering gold and copper. The theater seated over a thousand patrons and boasted a state-of-the-art audio system. Just listening to the orchestra warming up sent chills down Mare's spine. The music wasn't familiar—it had a foreign, Middle Eastern sound—but even the concordant notes the musicians struck as they tuned their instruments simultaneously had an other-worldly beauty.

"Wow." Mare had never seen anything like this before.

Elaine smiled. An usher handed them each a program and showed them to their seats. The cover of the program featured an icon of Mary of Egypt and Zosimas. They quickly read the Composer's Note before the overture began, which was penned by John Tavener.

Mary's door was wide open, even though her love was misdirected and distorted …

They looked at each other as they read, and then continued to read the rest of the program notes. Mare wondered how the words were hitting Elaine. She remembered how uncomfortable Elaine had been when they visited the Coptic church. *What's she thinking now?*

Zosimas's whole sound world becomes Mary's. In her he sees 'love' and his own limitations. His world, once so dry, now in the dryness of the desert, flowers into what the Desert Fathers might have called "Uncreated Eros" or a hint of the Edenic state. In controlled ecstasy, they both ask each other to give the blessing.

"That's what's happening in your painting, isn't it?" Elaine whispered.

Mare nodded and they continued reading Taverner's comments:

"Mary of Egypt" is the intent to create an ikon in sound about Non-Judgement. In a sense, Zosimas loves again when through Mary he can dimly see the beauty of God—and who knows how far Mary has gone in her search for the unknowable and unobtainable in her forty solitary years in the desert? Holy Mary, pray to God for us.

The orchestra finished warming up and the lights dimmed. A group of women and men formed two parallel lines on the stage, representing the extensions of Mary and Zosimas. The women's sensual movements were accompanied by a flute, wordlessly representing Mary whoring in Alexandria. The men were accompanied by the trombone and the primordial sound of the simantron—a wooden percussion instrument used in liturgical music (especially at monasteries) and sometimes with contemporary classical pieces. Each act was more powerful than the previous, building to a climax with the aria, "Bless." The characters of Zosimas and Mary—without their extensions from early scenes—prostrated themselves on the ground in front of each other, crying out in song the solitary word, "Bless!" over and over.

Mare wasn't prepared for how this would hit her—seeing the story she was growing more fascinated with by the day brought to life in such a powerful way on the stage. She felt some of the anger she'd hung onto over the years melt away as the words and music worked to soften her heart. *Damn.* She quickly brushed away tears, hoping Elaine hadn't seen them. Sneaking a glance at Elaine, Mare saw that she wasn't the only one weeping.

Then Mary levitated. The angels lifted her up—with help from nearly invisible wires hung from the stage ceiling—leaving a terrified and awestruck Zosimas to grieve her loss. The opera continued with the conclusion of their story: Zosimas found Mary dead in the desert a year later and buried her with help from a lion, who appeared tame in the presence of the saint's remains.

Leaving the opera, Elaine reached for Mare's hand. "You need to go to that monastery."

Elaine's touch felt good—like a sweet aunt or a grandmother—someone she could trust. It was a new feeling for Mare, and she didn't pull her hand away.

"Oh, I'm so glad you understand. There's a workshop in the spring that hasn't filled yet. I think it's during spring break so I wouldn't miss class."

"I don't think that even matters at this point, Mare. You need to do this. We'll have plenty of time for class when you get back."

"Thank you, Elaine." She gripped her mentor's hand tightly before letting go, her mind already racing ahead as she began to imagine visiting the monastery and learning to write icons.

Monasteries and Weeping Icons

Excerpt from *Cherry Bomb* (a novel)

Chapter 15

Mare wished it was already tomorrow morning and she was sitting in the
icon workshop, beginning to learn iconography. She would be comfortable there—in a studio setting—doing art. Tonight her thoughts were
painful. She unpacked her things into the small bureau and changed
into a skirt and blouse she'd found in a Savannah thrift shop. Her hands
shook as she tied a scarf around her hair. She was craving a smoke but
knew there wasn't time to dash down to the road before the service
began. Catching a glimpse of herself in the mirror, she wondered who
the hell *that* girl was. She darted from the guesthouse at the sound of the
bells tolling the evening vigil and the evocative tones of the talanton—
the long wooden bar and mallet used to summon the nuns to church
the way Noah called the animals to the ark. She remembered reading
about the talanton in James Taverner's notes from the opera program
and thought of Elaine for a second.

The sound stirred something in her heart:

To TAL an ton to TAL an ton to TA to TA to TAL an ton.

She hurried into the darkened chapel, nearly tripping over the
curled edge of a worn, knotted pile rug. As her eyes adjusted to the
candlelight, she noticed an icon on a stand in the middle of the nave.
A candle stand beside it was full of shimmering tapers. She found an
empty chair among the other visitors and started to sit down, but everyone was standing. An older woman next to her whispered, "That's
the weeping icon of Saint Mary of Egypt. Do you want to put a candle

there and ask her prayers?"

Mare looked closer at the icon and saw how much it looked like those in the churches in Macon and Atlanta—the same semi-naked image of a woman with sunbaked skin and long white hair. But this icon had a clear acrylic container attached to its base. The container appeared to be filling with a liquid, which dripped slowly from the icon.

"What is that—in the container?" Mare asked the woman.

"Her tears. It's a miracle. They say she's weeping sweet myrrh. Go ahead. Venerate it—here, I'll show you."

Before Mare could object, the woman took her by the arm and they moved closer to the icon. The woman crossed herself and kissed the icon on Saint Mary's right hand. Then she stepped aside and nodded at Mare, handing her a candle.

"Light it from one of the other tapers and place it in the sand. Saint Mary will pray for you."

Mare's hand was shaking. She lit the candle from the flames and placed it among the others, increasing their brilliance by one. Then she followed the woman back to their seats. Nuns in black habits were now assembled along the far side of the nave: three at the readers' stand, the rest in various states of prostration—some on their knees and curled into little black balls, their faces to the ground, hands tucked under their foreheads. No flesh was visible, no sign of their womanhood. Mare adjusted her own head covering, tucking strands of hair under the edges of the scarf. Her fingers tugged clumsily at the fabric, pulling it over her ears.

The scene could have been playing out in ancient Romania or Greece or Russia. But this was 1984, Mare thought, and she was in an Orthodox monastery in the mountains of North Carolina. How surreal! Her eyes searched the faces of the sisters as they rose from their prostrations to sing the evening hymns. The sun made its final appearance of the day, shooting polygons of light through the amber panes of the narrow, deep-set windows in the chapel and illumining the gold leaf halos of the icons and the faces of the nuns. Even their ears and the lower parts of their chins were covered by the black habits, so that only inverted triangles of flesh were visible, like white theatrical masks. No traces of makeup smoothed the blemishes of the young or the wrinkles of the old.

Yet Mare saw a subtle, clear-eyed beauty that emanated from each one. No colorful gloss plumped their lips, which appeared small and turned in on themselves. They were like the mouths painted on the icons that filled the walls of the chapel, quivering on the verge of Mona Lisa smiles as though they had just tasted something delicious or were trying to keep a secret.

And then there was this whole business of kissing things. Icons. Crosses. Relics. Even the hands of the abbess and the priest. The visitors' instructions in the guesthouse were pretty clear: *No lipstick, please. No bare arms, legs, or feet.* Mare tugged at the sleeves of her blouse, tucked her bare, sandal-clad feet under her chair (were they serious about the sock rule?) and closed her eyes. Breathing in the otherworldly aroma of the incense and the oil burning in the lampadas, she hushed the voices in her head and was left with the sound of silence. She could hear her heart beating, physically, in her chest. And then another voice cut through the rarified atmosphere, a voice at once familiar and strange, full of depth and quiet confidence. And reverence. One of the nuns had begun to read.

"The Life of our Holy Mother Mary of Egypt. Mother, bless the reading."

The nun bowed toward the abbess, who made the sign of the cross above her head and offered her hand for a kiss.

"*It is good to hide the secret of a king, but it is glorious to reveal and preach the works of God.'* So said the Archangel Raphael to Tobit when he performed the wonderful healing of his blindness. Actually, not to keep the secret of a king is perilous and a terrible risk, but to be silent about the works of God is a great loss for the soul. And I—says Saint Sophronius, in writing the life of Saint Mary of Egypt—am afraid to hide the works of God by silence ..."

Mare temporarily forgot herself as the words floated across the room, borne on their passage, it seemed, by mystical forces. It was the same story Father Mark had told her in Atlanta, but it seemed much more vivid tonight when read as part of a church service. The discomfort with her clothing—her wayward hair escaping the scarf, the nakedness of her toes—fell away from the edges of her consciousness, clearing her mental palette for new colors, preparing the canvas of her heart for new images. Her senses were aroused by the incense, the candlelight on egg tempera icons, the talantons, the bells, and now ... that voice.

Where have I heard that voice before?

As the nun continued to read the story of Mary of Egypt, Mare listened with rapt attention to the graphic details—many of which Father Mark had left out of Mary's wanton life in Egypt, where she lived as a prostitute.

"Every abuse of nature I regarded as life." The nun read these words and others that described her depravity. As she read, several of the nuns made prostrations, crossing themselves and weeping quietly. Even some visitors were moved to tears by the story. Especially the part where Mary was finally allowed to enter the church to venerate the true cross and, at the end, when the lion licked Mary's feet and helped Zossima bury her.

The nun finished the reading. All the others stood and sang hymns to this woman, Mary of Egypt, who was canonized by the

Church for her repentance and her ascetic struggles and the miracles she wrought.

> *Having been a sinful woman,*
> *You became through repentance a Bride of Christ.*
> *Having attained angelic life,*
> *You defeated demons with the weapon of the Cross.*
> *Therefore, most glorious Mary, You are a Bride of the Kingdom!*
> *Therefore your spirit, Holy Mother Mary, rejoices with the an-*
> *gels!*

Afterward, the abbess led the nuns in venerating the weeping icon. Father Zossima stood beside it holding a small brush, which he dipped in the "tears" as they streamed into the container. Then he anointed each worshipper by making the sign of the cross on their fore-heads and on the backs and the palms of their hands saying, "For the healing of soul and body."

When the woman next to Mare nudged her to go forward for the anointing, Mare whispered, "But what if I don't believe? I'm not Orthodox—I'm here to take an icon class. And even if God does exist, well, I'm pretty mad at Him right now."

The woman smiled. "God knows." And she gave Mare another gentle nudge.

As Mare approached the icon she thought she smelled roses, but she hadn't seen any roses in the chapel. Father Zossima smiled as he touched the brush to her forehead and made two short strokes, one vertical and one horizontal. She wanted to run, but she couldn't move.

Father Zossima leaned forward and spoke softly. "Your hands, please?"

Mare offered her hands, palms down and then palms up, as she had seen the others before her do. She watched, as if in a trance, while Father Zossima anointed them with the fragrant oil. She breathed in the aroma. Another drop of oil fell into the container.

It was the last thing Mare remembered before she hit the floor.

A Soft Opening
2008

My peonies didn't come out
For Pascha this year.
Well, one of them did—
The matriarch peeked through
Her dark green casing just enough to see,
Just enough to test the warmth of the sun
On her blossoming inner petals.

That's where the nymphs live—
Those mischievous fairies
For whom the plant is called
Shame,
Or Bashfulness
In the Language of Flowers.

Named for Paeon—
Physician to the Gods on Mount Olympus—
Who was gifted with the flower by the
Mother of Apollo, but then
Turned into one himself by
Warring factions amongst the gods,
The men gods, I might add.

Her seeds flew across cultures to become
A national emblem in China

Where she's known as the
Flower of Riches and Honor.
Then to Japan where her root was used
To treat convulsions in kampo—
A Japanese nod (yes) to Chinese medicine.

So this Bright Week I keep watching
For her blossoms to unfold,
But they keep waiting for the sun
To warm the air, to tease them
Into dancing—uninhibited—
In their birthday suits
In my front yard.

Maybe they're camera-shy,
Afraid of what my lens might reveal
To the world of poets and bloggers
And voyeurs, like me and Annie Leibovitz,
Too eager to reveal the hidden beauty
Of our subjects to the lusty, waiting world.

Shame on you, Billy Ray,
Lying there with your baby girl
As Annie's lens opens her budding
Maidenhood before the nymphs
Are ready for their coming out—
Before they are strong enough to
Bear the scrutiny of the watching world.

Shame on me, exposing the buds
Of my young peony bush too soon,
Impatient to see their beauty,
To smell their heady perfume
And to touch their tissue-soft
Petals before they are ready
For my embrace.

Maybe I'll wait for their
Grand Opening,
But more than likely
I'll be ready with my Lumix—
The aperture low—for a soft opening
Tomorrow, on May Day, in honor of Flora,
The Roman Goddess of flowers...
A convenient excuse
For my premature indulgence.

Wide Margins
2007

Marginalized.
That's what they call them—
Those people who find the edges
Of society too sharp to navigate
Without cutting something crucial
In the process.

Outsider artists.
That's the official category
Of the clients whose work hangs
In one of the swankiest galleries
In Seaside, Florida, so I asked
Outside of what?

The artists, she said
Are homeless, or schizophrenic
Or bipolar, or just poor
Or even Black, and that
Makes them
Outsider artists.

It seems the margins
Have gotten wider in the art world
While they continue to come under
Narrow scrutiny by the

Formatters of society, especially
In the South.

The trick, it seems,
Is to declare yourself—
Find a niche, a category where people
Won't feel uncomfortable about you
And a field where the margins
Are larger than life.

Nice work
If you can find it—
Most of us will have to trod along
In our pre-formatted pages just
Hoping that our sentences won't be
Too long for the margins.

VI

MENTAL HEALTH, ADDICTION, AND SEXUAL ABUSE

Until we have been healed, we do not know what wholeness is: the discipline of creation, be it to paint compose, or write, is an effort towards wholeness. . . . The important thing is to remember that our gift, no matter what the size, is indeed something given us and which we must humbly serve, and in serving, learn more wholeness, be offered wondrous newness.

—Madeleine L'Engle

Sobriety—it's about more than not being drunk. It's clear-eyed brush strokes and poetry that knocks your socks off and page-turning prose. It's Iris Dement singing, "I choose to take my sorrow straight," and Natalie Maines (of the Dixie Chicks) turning a personal affront into a hit song with, "I'm Not Ready to Make Nice." It's Mary Chapin Carpenter singing, "forgiveness doesn't come with a debt." But it's also allowing yourself to be human, and turning that broken humanity into something redemptive with every stroke of your pen or brush or keyboard.

—Susan Cushman, *from "Blocked" (Santa Fe Writers Project, literary awards finalist, July 2, 2008)*

Eat, Drink, Repeat: One Woman's (Three-Day) Search for Everything

2013

Tuesday morning, 7:30 a.m. Paul Newman's Special Blend Organic Decaf K-Cup goes into the Keurig brewer. Eight ounces of steaming java flow into the white mug with the blue logo from Square Books in Oxford, Mississippi, on one side, and a quote from Winnie the Pooh Goes Visiting on the other. Remember the scene where Pooh ate too much and got stuck in the hole in the tree, so he asked Christopher Robin to comfort him? *Then would you read a Sustaining Book, such as would help and comfort a Wedged Bear in Great Tightness?* Breathing in the full-bodied aroma from the handpicked Arabica beans, I stir in three packets of raw sugar until they completely dissolve and add a quick pour of Land O'Lakes fat free half-and-half. Seventy calories and zero grams of fat. Not as sustaining as a Caramel Macchiato from Starbucks, which I gave up after I discovered that each grande Caramel Macchiato (without whipped cream) has 240 calories and 7 grams of fat. With whip? Add another 5 to 11 grams of fat.

8:30 a.m. Frosted Cheerios make a sound like an old-fashioned bicycle bell as they tumble into a cornflower blue ceramic bowl with a terra-cotta glaze on the inside. A few ounces of fat-free milk moisten the tiny donuts just enough to set the sugar-coating free but not enough to subdue the crunch each bite delivers, temporarily satisfying the craving triggered by a life-long eating disorder known as *pica*. (Crunching on these cholesterol-fighting nuggets is certainly preferable to ice—which ruins teeth—and clay and other non-food items, long buried in my past.) The method of delivery is an eighteen-gauge Towle Beaded Antique oval soupspoon, which has a nice heft, even when only filled with cereal. After licking the last drops of sugary-sweet milk from the glossy mirrored bowl of the spoon, I am greeted by my image in reverse—turned on my head by my first encounter with food this morning, and already thinking about what comes next.

9:30 a.m. Writing, laundry, writing, bills, writing, Facebook, writing, email. Diversionary tactics only keep the cravings at bay for brief intervals. By mid-morning I remember that McDonald's quits serving breakfast at 10:30 a.m. A mere three blocks separate my kitchen from theirs and the sizzling, greasy sausages snuggled into those buttery biscuits. Rule #1: Only eat sausage biscuits on road trips. After ten-thirty those succulent baby sandwiches are replaced by French fries—tossed around in hot, oily baskets with a blizzard of salt covering every surface of each morsel—the fast food that changed a generation of taste buds forever. Rule #2: Never order French fries. Ever. By 10:30 I have managed to keep my body out of the kitchen for an hour, but my mind is anywhere but on the work at hand. Except that today I'm actually writing about food.

10:30 a.m. I've been awake for three hours with no protein or salt. Generously salted scrambled eggs cooked well-done in real butter like an overly bothered omelet satisfies both needs. But the salt makes me thirsty and the protein doesn't act quickly enough for the instant blood sugar boost I'm craving, so I wash them down with a few sips of ice cold canned Coke. I open one can a day and sip on it for about twenty-four hours—my replacement for diet colas, preferring quality to quantity. I was so excited when the new six-ounce cans came out—the ones shaped like tiny little Red Bulls—because of the way they feel in my hand, and they help me cut down on calories. Or at least that's the plan. The edge of the can has an almost sensual feel on my lips as the quintessential caramel-colored thirst-quencher glides down my throat, delivering a refreshing carbonated rush. But as I finish washing the saucepan and putting my dishes away, the craving only grows stronger. *Sugar. Chocolate.* I scoop a couple of dips of Edy's Slow-Churned Rich & Creamy vanilla ice cream—the kind with half the fat, of course—into a stemless martini glass. Next I drizzle Hershey's chocolate syrup over the ice cream, enough to assure chocolate to the last bite. This time a Towle teaspoon delivers the goods, its smaller shape being more efficient at scraping out the final bits of chocolate syrup that cling to the bottom. When the spoon doesn't do the job, I use my tongue. By now the morning is nearly gone. I've achieved very little real work, and shame sets in.

11:30 a.m. How many times do I look at the clock, waiting for permission to pour that first drink? Some days I make it until afternoon. But not today. I realize I haven't stopped eating, drinking, or thinking about eating and drinking all morning. I don't need the bathroom scales to tell me I'm at my all-time heaviest weight. My clothes remind me each time I shed my stretchy yoga pants for jeans or my baggy T-shirt for a fitted blouse. I've put away close to a thousand calories before noon, with plans to prepare a nice oven-roasted pork tenderloin, baked sweet potatoes and fresh Brussels sprouts for dinner. None of those foods appeal to me, but they are favorites of my husband and daughter. I already know that I will sit down to dinner and only nibble at the nutritional fare my body really needs. By seven tonight I'll be full, but still not satisfied. And so at 11:45 this morning I pour a glass of Monkey Bay Sauvignon Blanc into a small pink Depression wine goblet I got at an antique store in Arkansas. It doesn't have the same feel as the larger, clear white wine goblets from William Sonoma, but I can't hide them in the dishwasher amongst the coffee mugs and juice glasses like I can the smaller glasses. I save the larger ones for evenings when my husband is imbibing with me. Anticipation builds with the sound of the cork leaving the bottle. The distinctive *chug chug chug* of the wine filling the glass. It's not really a cork—it's a rubber wine stopper (from Rabbit) and its phallic shape and texture is tempting. I place it in my mouth and suck the last drops of wine from its surface as I slowly pull it away and push it back into the bottle. The first swallow is always the best, bringing instant gratification, holding promises of relief, of edges softening, jaws relaxing, mind slowing down, dark clouds abating. And sometimes it makes good on those promises, but the relief is only temporary. Even now as I'm penning these words, the afternoon has begun and a second glass of wine is calling.

12:30 p.m. My husband's perma-press shirts and khaki pants are washed, dried, and hung, wrinkle-free, in his closet—mindless work that somehow soothes because I can be successful in this endeavor. I love the way the Egyptian cotton feels and smells as I rescue his shirts from the dryer. The comfort is short-lived, as my minds returns to food, and to the fact that everything I've eaten today has either been simple carbohydrates or protein. Not one of the recommended five daily servings of fruits or vegetables has graced my lips, unless you count wine as a fruit, in which case I'm now on my second serving. I look around the kitchen and find fresh peaches ripening in a small brown bag on the counter. I pull one out and make a small indentation in its flesh with my thumb—it feels ripe. I bring the fuzzy yellow-red orb to my nose (I always smell my food before tasting it) and breathe in its sweet aroma. It's ready. Using a small, white-handled Cutco paring knife, I make one incision, then another, allowing a perfect slice to be removed from the peach. I observe its texture—free of pithiness—and its color: red tendrils, freshly pulled from the seed, contrast with the shiny yellow crescent. I put the entire slice into my mouth and savor it slowly. I give it an 8. If it were a 10, I would eat the rest of the peach naked. Instead, I pour a small amount of white sugar into a saucer and dip the remaining slices, one at a time, into the sugar before eating them. No longer savoring the flavor, I eat mindlessly, reaching into the bag for another peach, dipping one slice after another into the sugar, waiting for a surge of energy and wondering if it will sustain me for an afternoon of writing and working out and preparing dinner.

1:30 p.m. A second glass of Monkey Bay carries me just past 1,500 words of this essay but the sugar high is over and the salt craving has returned with a vengeance. *Chips.* I want chips with guacamole (that's a fruit, right?) or cheese dip. But if I go there, will I make it upstairs to work out? I hurry to the elliptical, rushing past the pantry and upstairs onto the machine that will help me burn some of those empty calories and hopefully shoot some much-needed endorphins into my nutritionally and chemically unbalanced system. I run down my list of recorded shows on TiVo and settle on last night's new episode of *Law and Order: SVU*, which requires a bit of mental energy to follow. I fast-forward through the commercials, assuring a food-free media session, although it's nearly impossible not to notice the butter dripping off the pasta in the Olive Garden spots, even at double fast-forward. I actually slow down to watch one of them, nearly drooling into my water bottle in the process.

2:30 p.m. Four and a half hours until dinner. Plenty of time to metabolize a snack first, right? A little queso dip into the microwave and a dozen or so crisp, salty tortilla chips from the pantry join me by the sink where I stand to eat them while watching more of my favorite TiVo-ed shows—this time it's an old episode of *House*. The queso is only "medium" but I don't do hot and spicy so it's burning my mouth just enough to push my margarita button. But I swore off making margaritas at home a long time ago, so I mix up a short Tanqueray and diet tonic with lime. My glass is a wonderful little oval-shaped number from Pottery Barn with wavy lines etched inside. I start with ice—to fill the glass about two-thirds to the top—and then squeeze the fresh lime over the ice, dropping the lime wedge into the glass. The gin comes next. I don't measure, but guess at the shot—1.5 to 2 ounces. The fizzy diet tonic brings it all to life. I can feel the carbonation tickle my nose as I pull the glass to my mouth, smell the lime and finally the Tanqueray. I celebrate the marriage of chips and queso with gin and tonic for about thirty minutes. And then it's over. I place my hand over my full belly, moving it across my disappearing waistline and running it quickly over my growing love handles. I consider purging, a practice I haven't outgrown from my teenage years. More shame sets in.

3:30 p.m. Two thousand calories in and three drinks under my belt, I face the computer screen and close my eyes. Maybe I need a nap. It's either that or another gin and tonic. I'm in no shape to work. The couch wins, and I allow myself the luxury of reading—not just for pleasure but also as research for my novel-in-progress. I'm fascinated by Michael Cunningham's book, *The Hours.* Lured into the interior worlds of Virginia Woolf, Clarissa Dalloway and '50s housewife Laura Brown for a while, I don't think of food, or drink, or my own insecurities. Until I get to the part where Laura Brown's husband leaves for work and she's left alone with her son and her responsibilities as a mother. "When her husband is here, she can manage it. She can see him seeing her…. Alone with the child, though, she loses direction. She can't always remember how a mother would act." Suddenly I remember that I'm alone, and like Laura Brown, my husband isn't here to see me, to remind me, if only by his presence, how to act. The familiar fog of disgrace creeps back in. I know I should get up and do something productive, but instead I find my way to the freezer for a Skinny Cow ice cream sandwich. Only 140 calories. I take the sandwich back to the couch and continue to read as I taste the cold, low-fat vanilla ice cream wrapped perfectly in the soft chocolate wafers, which stick to my fingers, requiring licking and sucking to get the bits of chocolate off my fingertips. The process distracts me from my reading, and I return to the freezer for another ice cream sandwich. And yes, a third one, tossing the empty container into the trash, burying it beneath the morning's cereal box.

5:30 p.m. Time to start dinner for my husband and daughter. I preheat the oven to 350 degrees for the pork tenderloin. Opening the refrigerator to get out the sprouts and sweet potatoes, I see the limes. Another gin and tonic will ease the discomfort of preparing a dinner that I'm too full to eat. A cocktail before dinner—what could be more benign? My husband and daughter arrive home from work. *Hi, honey, I'm home. Kiss. How was your day? Oh, fine. Mmm, supper smells delicious, what is it? Pork tenderloin, Brussels sprouts and baked sweet potatoes. Aren't you joining us, Mom?* Hug. She grabs a Stella from the fridge and he mixes a Vodka and 7 with lemon. *No, I'm really not hungry, and besides, I kind of snacked all day.* Husband and daughter both smile. *But I'll sit and have a drink and visit with you guys while you eat.* The Brussels sprouts' tiny leaves are bright green and glistening. Brown sugar and butter dissolve into the rich orange flesh of the sweet potatoes. Mustard and honey drip from the skin of the pork tenderloin. Nutritionally and aesthetically balanced. *So what did you do today, dear? I wrote an essay about food.*

8:30 p.m. The evening is filled with talk of our daughter's impending move to Colorado and plans for her wedding next spring. And my trip to Denver in a week to visit our son and meet my new granddaughter, two weeks old. Our daughter is leaving the nest—forever—in two days. So tomorrow afternoon we have appointments for mother-daughter manicures and pedicures at The Nail Bar down in Harbor Town, followed by drinks at Tug's Grill on the Mississippi River. Later we'll meet her dad at our favorite sushi restaurant downtown.

11:30 p.m. My husband sleeps soundly beside me. Our daughter is upstairs. Probably on the phone with her fiancé or watching a movie on her computer. The lonely silence beckons me out of the bedroom.

It feels like I'm sleepwalking to the kitchen. I open the refrigerator and find the Monkey Bay from earlier this afternoon. About one-third full. I twist off the top and consider which glass to fill. Fuck that. I put the bottle to my lips, empty it in four swigs, and toss it into the trash. I reach under the cabinet for a new bottle and put it in the refrigerator for tomorrow.

Wednesday morning, 7:30 a.m. My sweet husband brings me coffee in bed, our usual morning routine. I remember as I awaken that today is the day. Our daughter is packing to move. But we have the afternoon at the Nail Bar to look forward to. Then drinks and sushi. The anticipation quells my hunger somewhat. And I'm not alone in the house today. There's someone here to see me, or as much as I'm willing to be seen. And so I spend the morning focusing on the delayed gratification of the afternoon and evening, which fills the emptiness. I avoid binging, work out on the elliptical, and make it through four hours without constant thoughts of food and drink. I write a blog post and answer emails, check out Facebook, breathe in and out. Find my way upstairs to the elliptical.

11:30 a.m. After a good workout I begin to feel physical hunger—a sensation I welcome, hoping it means that my metabolism is catching up with yesterday's mother lode of calories. My husband comes home for lunch, my daughter finishes her pre-move errands, and we enjoy a light fare of pita bread, hummus and fresh peaches. I toast the pita with a thin smearing of softened butter, cut it into triangles, and arrange them around the pine nut hummus, which has been dipped into lotus bowls. The cold, smooth olive-oil-topped hummus contrasts perfectly with the buttery pita points. It all washes down smoothly with half a can of Coke. And yes, it would be better with a glass of wine, but we'll be at the bar by four-thirty or five, right? Time to get back to the essay at hand. The next couple of hours are absorbed with writing and occasional interruptions from my daughter as she continues to pack for her move.

1:45 p.m. Time to shower. By this time yesterday I was on my third drink, so what could it hurt to have a small glass of wine while I'm showering and dressing for the afternoon and evening? *Twisted.* That's my favorite pinot grigio, and the open bottle in the fridge is hard to avoid. My husband has gone back to work and my daughter is running errands. *Chug chug chug* flows the fruity white liquid into a disposable plastic cup—easier to manage in the bathroom. The first sip of the day is always magical. I carry the cup into the shower with me, but it's gone before I can rinse the shampoo from my hair, and I dry off quickly, thirsty for a refill. A second pour accompanies my after-shower routine. By 2:45 I'm ready to leave for the Nail Bar, with only about 600 calories consumed.

4:30 p.m. Manicures and pedicures are done and we're off to Tug's Grill. It's still too hot to enjoy the patio so we head straight to the bar. The top-shelf margarita awakens my cravings as I sip it slowly over the next thirty minutes while enjoying my last outing with my daughter before she moves away.

5:15 p.m. We meet my husband at Blue Fin for sushi. He's a few minutes late, so we get started with a beer for my daughter and a glass of Ferrari-Carano fume blanc for me. Peppery aromas of lime zest and lemongrass are complemented by the crisp freshness of grapefruit and a deeper suggestion of ripe pear. (Okay, I read that on the label, but only after I picked up on those scents and flavors myself.) After my husband joins us, we enjoy five different sushi rolls and conversation that's a bit sentimental and void of very much day-to-day chatter. It is, after all, our last dinner with our daughter before she moves to Denver to be with her fiancé. The Lobster Roll is my favorite; the Dragon Roll runs a close second. My daughter compliments my improved skills with the chopsticks since our last sushi outing and I remind her that it's only one of many skills she has taught me over the years. I touch each piece of roll lightly into the soy sauce dish before placing the entire morsel into my mouth. Crunching down on the festival of flavors and textures in each tiny masterpiece is like a private party for the taste buds. Eating and drinking slowly tonight, savoring the moment, I find that I am full before finishing the rolls, and I skip dessert, taking only a taste of my husband's trio of ice creams when they arrive. I finish the day somewhere under 1,500 calories, and without my usual feelings of bloatedness and guilt. Back home, I crawl in bed around nine, knowing that I'll be up at five-thirty to take my daughter to the airport. Around nine-thirty she plops down on the bed beside me for a "last night at home" chat. When she leaves the room, around ten, my soul—and my belly—are full and I quickly fall asleep.

Thursday, 5:30 a.m. There's only time for one cup of coffee before driving my daughter to the airport. The drive is lovely, with the sun coming up across the expanse of the runways. We don't talk much, but there's a lot of feeling in the air. We hug goodbye, knowing we'll see each other in a couple of weeks when I fly out to visit my son and his family, so the parting doesn't feel like forever. Until I get back into the car and look over my shoulder at this beautiful young woman pulling her suitcases through the glass doors of the airport and out of this phase of our lives, forever. I make it a few blocks away from the airport before turning into a McDonald's for a sausage biscuit—a replacement for the one I managed to avoid on Tuesday. I only eat around the outside of the sandwich, where the biscuit is brown and the sausage is well-cooked, tossing the soggier center bite into the bag. The fountain Coke on ice cools my throat, as I weep most of the way home. By the time I arrive I pull myself together and greet my husband cheerfully.

6:30 a.m. He's getting ready for work, but we briefly discuss our plans for the evening. We're going to the twelfth-annual *Memphis Business Journal's* Health Care Heroes Awards banquet because he is one of the twenty nominees up for five awards. He has been nominated for the "Health Care Heroes in Innovation" award. The other three nominees have sexier platforms (children's cancer treatments and surgical devices, biomedical engineering devices) than his nearly four decades of research in hypertension, so he doesn't expect to win. I'm used to accompanying him to medical meetings. I've been doing it for almost forty years. In May I went with him to Washington, D.C., where he was presented with a national research award. I often eat or drink too much at these events, out of nervousness, anxiety, and feelings of insecurity in the company of so many brilliant and accomplished people. As soon as he leaves for work I begin a familiar cycle.

8:30 a.m. It starts innocuously enough, with a bowl of fresh peaches I cut up the night before. They're a little mushier than they were when I first cut them on Wednesday, and the sugar I sprinkled on them has melted into a syrup, leaving me wanting the texture of the crystals. If not sugar, salt. I recognize the danger signals and hurry away from the kitchen to the computer, replacing the fix with an hour spent on Facebook and email before returning to the essay at hand.

10:30 a.m. I go upstairs into my daughter's empty room, and the tears start up again. I hug her stuffed animals, one at a time—the bears, and especially the blue dolphin—and sit on the edge of her bed. Only a few books remain on her shelves and some remnants of her life with us are still tucked away in her closet. She lived in this room for the past three summers during graduate school, while she worked for an architectural firm in West Memphis, Arkansas. Other than that, it had been nine years since she left us for college and a couple of years of working before grad school. But these three summers were the best times for us as mother and daughter, and now I want to hold those memories close forever. I take her towels downstairs to the laundry room and picture the new life she's moving on to, and I hope that she will find everything she wants in her marriage, her family, and her career. My tears have awakened my hunger and I head into the kitchen.

11:30 a.m. It starts with chips and guacamole—homemade with fresh avocados and tomatoes from the farmer's market, a squirt of lime and salt. I finish the bowl with about a third of a bag of chips, washing them down with Coke. In the background I play some old episodes of *Glee* that I've recorded, mainly listening to the show tunes as I continue my binge. Next up is a grilled cheese sandwich. First I melt a few tablespoons of real butter in the skillet. I dip a piece of bread in the butter, put it on top of the cheese, and place the sandwich into the butter with the bare side of the bread down. It smells sweet as it sizzles, and I turn it to check the patterns of brown and yellow on the other side. When it's done I cut it on the diagonal and spread sweet pickle relish on top (something I learned from a friend in my Mississippi childhood) and take it with me into the den. I eat it in front of the television, which mutes the enjoyment and numbs my mental alertness.

12:30 p.m. Making another attempt at writing pulls me back into reality and I realize what I've just done. The sadness leads me to the refrigerator for my first glass of wine for the day. I'm back to Savignon Blanc now, and I go through two glasses fairly quickly, bringing my calorie count to around 1,200 by the middle of the day. In a few short hours I'll be dressing up for the awards banquet, sitting nervously by my husband's side, meeting and greeting the other medical professionals and their spouses. Trying on several pairs of shoes before the mirror in our bedroom—like a little girl playing dress up—I set out the black heels. But I don't feel pretty. After binging all day on chips and grilled cheese and sausage biscuit and wine, the self-hatred drives me to my knees once again. But not in prayer. My reflection in the bottom of the toilet bowl—and a fetid memory long ago encoded in my frontal lobe—are enough to trigger my seasoned gag reflex. This ritual takes less than a minute. I puke up most of what I've eaten in the past couple of hours. It brings relief, but not without more self-loathing. I cannot, as James Baldwin urged, "vomit the anguish up."

2:30 p.m. I need to work out, shower and get ready for the evening. I allow myself half a can of Coke, to quell the after burn from vomiting and to soothe my esophagus and stomach.

6:00 p.m. We arrive halfway through the cocktail reception. I have a gin and tonic, which I carry with me into the banquet at six-thirty. There's been a mix-up in the seating arrangements, and our friends fill a round table for ten, leaving us to sit with one single man at another table, alone, just us three. Feeling embarrassed and left out, I slip back out to the cash bar for another gin and tonic. Anxious to get off my feet—why did I wear these fucking heels?—I return to my seat at our near-empty table. When the food arrives, I nibble at the flattened chicken breast, cold pasta and overcooked vegetables. Even the key lime pie—my favorite dessert—isn't very good, so I leave most of it on the plate as I continue to glance awkwardly at the seven empty places at our table, wondering if the looks I'm receiving from others in the room are ones of sympathetic embarrassment. When the program begins, the twenty nominees' pictures are put up on two screens in the room as each one's bio is read. The crowd—about two hundred and fifty people—stands and applauds as each winner receives his award. When the third award is announced, we hear my husband's name spoken from the platform in the front of the room: "William Cushman." All the eyes in the room are on us as we stand and I kiss him, and he makes his way from our mostly empty table in the back corner to the stage up front. His brief acceptance "speech," handshakes, and photo ops fill the next few minutes, and as he returns to me, a number of our friends at the next table come over with their congratulatory hugs and smiles.

8:30 p.m. On the drive home, we talk about the award and my husband's surprise. He's a humble man who works quietly under the radar, enhancing and saving the lives of millions of people with high blood pressure all over the world on a daily basis. I love him and I'm proud of him, but the evening has been difficult. As we watch the 10 p.m. news (hey—there's Joe Birch, Channel 5 anchor, who was emcee at the awards banquet) the gin and tonics wear off and I pour two fingers of Crown over ice for my husband and two for me. I fight back the tears as I sit in the den with him. My husband's success can't touch the dark recesses of my damaged spirit, but only adds to the clutter of our life's minutiae. As he retreats to the bedroom after the news, I pick up *The Hours* from the coffee table and continue to read.

The Princess and the Witch

(A chapter from an unpublished memoir, *Dressing the Part: What I Wore For Love*)

It's not unusual for a girl raised in the South to be obsessed with clothing. Just visit the university campuses of the South East Conference for a fashion and beauty pageant unparalleled in other parts of the country. Growing up in Mississippi in the 1950s and '60s was difficult enough for the girl whose self-esteem was intact. But for one whose innocence was stolen by those she should have been able to trust—first in her family and later in her community—the devastation is swift and the damage remains throughout her life. The betrayal inherent in incest causes the child to go into such distress that she ends up using methods of rescue for herself that are as damaging as the abuse itself. Self-contempt. Eating disorders. Body image distortion. Substance abuse. And yes, even an obsession with something as seemingly benign as clothing.

For me, the abuse started when I was only four years old. And my first efforts at reclaiming my lost sense of beauty were thwarted by my third grade teacher.

Another piece of my heart died the day Mrs. Tennyson announced the parts for our third grade play. I stayed after school to plead with her. I was desperate to be the princess, but she insisted that the witch had more lines. All the princess did was smile and wave her wand.

Jan McMillan was perfect for that role, with her long, blond hair and pre-pubescent Barbie doll smile. Her only flaw was that her teeth were slightly too large for her mouth. An eight-year-old Farrah Fawcett dressed in a beautiful taffeta gown with sparkly sequins. *But she's not the star*.

That's what I kept telling myself as I walked the short half-block home from school, trying to dry my tears before facing my mother with the news. She was in the kitchen, washing turnip greens in the sink, when I walked in.

I grabbed an apple and plopped down at the breakfast bar. Mother stopped washing the greens and looked at me, her eyebrows pulling her face up into a hopeful question mark. The silence hung heavily between us. Finally I mumbled, fighting back tears, "Jan McMillan is the princess."

"And you?"

"The witch."

Mother returned to the greens in the sink. "Well, I'm sure Mamaw can make a witch costume for you that will be beautiful. And you know, black is very slimming."

Her efforts to soothe my disappointment were lost on my skinny eight-year-old self. My mother is a beautiful, petite, woman, even now at eighty-five. She was stunning in her thirties, when she was dressing me for school plays, piano recitals and birthday parties.

Mamaw was my grandmother—my mother's mother. She made almost all my clothes, including costumes. I rode the Trailways bus from Jackson, Mississippi to her home in Meridian for my final costume fitting, the weekend before the play. As I stood in front of the mirror in her sewing room, watching her pin up the hem for my black witch's dress, I tried to imagine the princess gown she would have made for me. I wiggled and shifted my hips and waved my imaginary wand in the air.

"Stand still, Susan. I'm almost finished." The straight pins she held between her teeth as she knelt on the floor beside me muffled her voice, always sweet and mild.

"But I hafta' go to the bathroom!"

She stood up, our eyes meeting—she was only four feet, eleven inches tall—and she gently pulled the black dress over my head, careful not to let the pins scratch my bare tummy and chest. I ran into the bathroom, wearing only my little girl panties, and lifted the cover on the toilet. It was the same spot where my grandfather had stood, four years earlier, when I walked in without knocking.

A strange mix of embarrassment and curiosity held me in the doorway, staring at Granddaddy and what he was doing in front of the toilet. I started to turn and leave, but he grabbed my arm and closed the door. Before I could get away, he pulled me over to his side and placed my hand on his body. With his hand on top of mine, he moved it up and down. I looked away just as he made a groaning sound, and then he let go of my hand and exhaled loudly.

I can't remember how often this happened. He died when I was five, but his ghost haunted that room, and that house where I would spend a decade of summer vacations with my grandmother, who lovingly sewed the garments in which my mother would dress me for all the parts I would play throughout childhood and adolescence.

I always thought those hand jobs were our dirty little secret, until I grew up and learned about how childhood abuse can distort a person's body image and sense of self, often leading to eating disorders and addictive behaviors. It certainly explains a lot about my mother.

As I entered adulthood, I began to ask her to tell me more about her father, about Granddaddy. Her stories were filled with his rules. She wasn't allowed to wear shorts outside the house. She wasn't allowed to go on dates in high school. She resorted to making up stories about spending the night with a girlfriend in order to meet boys at the skating rink or the movie. She was an only child, with a mousy little mother to protect her from her father's tyrannical ways. Although she never mentioned him ever touching her, her obsessions with weight and appearance—hers and mine—and later her alcoholism, were telltale signs.

Families and friends filled the auditorium as fifty or sixty third-graders scurried around behind the curtain, making last-minute adjustments to costumes and scenery. Court jesters in bright striped tunics practiced twirling ribbons in the air on the ends of wooden dowels. Maids-in-waiting pranced around, comparing their colorful, satiny dresses and giggling at the boys who had to wear tights under their medieval bloomers. I took one last look at my reflection in the backstage mirror, covered from head to toe in black, and knew that if I was going to be the star, somehow I would have to *be the color*.

The only palette available to me on that stage at Pearl Spann Elementary School in 1959 was my voice. Standing front and center with the spotlight on my face, I spoke my lines with the intensity and abandon of an artist throwing paint on a canvas—splashes of red, splatters of green, bold strokes of yellow came gushing from my mouth. The rush I got from the realization that the audience was listening to my words almost made me forget what I was wearing. Until the Princess entered from stage right. Her brightness stung my heart, like a target-seeking missile, locking onto the hole, which hid beneath the black witch's robe. The hole that had been put there by my grandfather.

I would try to fill that hole with substitutes for decades to come. Or cover it with clothes that made me feel beautiful, and loved. *What I wore* at every stage of my life was more than a fashion or political statement, and more than a reflection of the culture. With each wardrobe change, I would add another layer, trying to cover my wounded psyche, longing for the day when I would finally be comfortable in my own skin. It would be a life-long struggle to dress the part—the *parts*—that would be cast for me by others. And later the parts I would choose for myself.

Six decades into the story, I still struggle against the belief that clothes make the woman, and that the holy grail of love and acceptance is somehow wrapped up in being beautiful. And thin. A counselor once told me there is lots of power in the beauty of a woman. That feminine beauty is evocative to all of us, bringing to light the intangible connectedness to each other, stirring up unconscious realms of magnificence we are usually detached from. But as amazingly good and valuable as the artistry of a lovely woman is, it's not enough to take care of darkness of this magnitude, of incest and sexual abuse. I may never get over the landslide of betrayal set up for me by this patriarch in my life.

In November of 2010 I met another writer who had experienced childhood incest. Robert Goolrick was reading from his memoir, *The End of the World As We Know It*, at a writing conference I helped direct in Oxford, Mississippi. Goolrick was raped by his father "just once" when he was a small boy and his father was drunk. His memoir describes, in the most powerful, dark, poetic prose I've ever read on the subject, the ongoing affects on the soul of the person who is violated in this way:

"If you don't receive love from the ones who are meant to love you, you will never stop looking for it, like an amputee who never stops missing his leg, like the ex-smoker who wants a cigarette after lunch fifteen years later. It sounds trite. It's true. You will look for it in objects that you buy without want. You will look for it in faces you do not desire. You will look for it in expensive hotel rooms, in the careful attentiveness of the men and women who change the sheets every day, who bring you pots of tea and thinly sliced lemon and treat you with false deference. … You will look for it in shop girls and the kind of sad and splendid men who sell you clothing. You will look for it and you will never find it. You will not find a trace."

I wept as he read. And yet I found it darkly comforting, listening to him read these words that explain why he decided to tell his story:

"I tell it because there is an ache in my heart for the imagined beauty of a life I haven't had, from which I have been locked out, and it never goes away."

The imagined beauty of a life I haven't had. Through all the wardrobe changes. Through all the roles I've played and continue to play.

The New Normal
2015

I'm writing this the day before the two-year anniversary of my car wreck. Looking back at last year's reflection, "It's All Grace," one thing hasn't changed: I still don't want to dwell on the accident itself. I still get a little creeped out when I hear or see an ambulance. Have I become a more careful driver? Sure. Do I want to watch the video of the wreck (compliments of the video cam on the front of the ambulance)? No. I have a copy of the DVD. It's in a thick file folder with all the paperwork from Sacred Heart Trauma Center in Pensacola, Florida. I pretty much have the rest of the contents of that folder memorized. It was such a relief when the insurance and medical bills were finally all settled, over a year after the wreck. There are lots of other folders in the same drawer—four different surgeons, two different physical therapy centers, home health services and equipment, etc. But those are just the details.

What I'm thinking about today is my life moving forward. Just over a month ago a friend had a terrible accident with a lawnmower and lost her big toe and a lot of skin, tissue and cartilage on her left foot. I spent some time with her in the hospital during the two weeks in which she had seven surgeries. She will have several more in the coming weeks and months. She's anxious about the future—what to expect looking forward. She's been told that it will be a year before she reaches her "new normal."

That got me to thinking about what my "new normal" looks like. I know that people mean well when they see me at church or elsewhere and say things like, "You look wonderful!" or "I'm so glad to see you back to normal." I guess I look "normal" because my injuries—unlike my friend who lost a toe—aren't so visible on the outside. You can't see the plates and nails and screws that are holding my neck and right leg and ankle together. You can't see the bumpy line of scar tissue where staples once repaired the gash on top of my head. You can't see my neck zipper because of my long hair. And of course you can't see the aches, pains and stiffness. But I can feel them. Every day. The trauma aggravated the arthritis that already plagued me before the wreck. And the months I spent in a hospital bed, then a wheelchair, walker, cast, boot, crutches, etc. played havoc with my hips and knees.

The *new normal* means that my neck gets tired of holding up my head. Although the average human head only weighs about 10-11 pounds, most days mine feels much heavier than that. It's difficult to spend hours writing at the computer or reading in a chair, and yet that's where most of my life is lived these days.

The *new normal* means that walking on pavement or sidewalks causes pain to my ankle. A casual stroll at sunset is okay. But exercise is confined to the elliptical (thankful I can do that!) and the occasional water workout in a neighbor's pool (which I love).

The *new normal* means that doing things that require a high level of energy—like planning and hosting parties, having company for dinner, being with grandchildren—are exhausting and challenging. But these are the things I love most so I push on.

The *new normal* means that I have a higher level of brain fuzz than before the wreck. Being 64 and possibly third generation Alzheimer's, I'm sure some of this is genetic. But I haven't recovered the same level of concentration I once had.

The *new normal* also means that *most days* I find a way to thank God for these struggles. Yes. The tiredness, aches and pains are there because (1) I am alive and (2) I'm not paralyzed. I hope I never take these realities for granted, although I know I must whenever I complain. My sweet husband bears the brunt of that, since most of the time I manage to put up a happy and healthy front when I'm away from the house. Or even when I'm home and entertaining. But when it's just the two of us, I'm afraid I often sound grumpy. I'm working on that, because no one should have to live with an ungrateful bitch.

The *new normal* means that I often try to numb my aches, pain and depression with comfort food. I currently weigh more than I ever have. Most of my pants and jeans are too tight and I've bought dresses and tops in larger sizes. From a mental health point of view, this bothers me more than the aches and pains. Issues with food and weight aren't new in my life. They're just exacerbated by my other struggles. I know enough about food and nutrition to make better choices, and I hope that I can incorporate those choices into the new normal for my life. One day at a time.

And finally, the *new normal* is a financial term describing the economic conditions in our country following the recession of 2007-2012. As a people, most of us don't want to deny ourselves the lifestyle we work hard to provide for ourselves and our families. We don't like to be disciplined in our consumer habits. And yet the reality is that there are consequences for our actions. We have to live with those consequences and learn to make better choices. This is especially hard for those of us who often buy things in an effort to comfort our suffering. I hope that putting these things in writing will help me embrace this part of my new normal as I move forward.

God Weeps
2015

Although many people were more interested in Pope Francis' words concerning immigration, homelessness and climate change in his first visit to the U.S., it was his meeting with victims of sexual abuse by church leaders that caused me to sit up and listen.

The Pope met with five survivors of abuse, assuring them that their abusers would be held accountable. And then he said this, publicly: *God weeps…. It continues to overwhelm me with shame that the people who were charged with taking care of these tender ones violated their trust and caused them tremendous pain.*

Although some activist groups and individual politicians say his words were just for a public display—and yes, action is needed to bring the perpetrators to justice—I believe they are words of healing. Probably because I'm one of the victims, although my abusers weren't clergy in the Catholic Church.

Two of the three men who molested me as a child and young adult asked my forgiveness. The third—my grandfather—died before I was old enough to confront him about what he did to me. His sin is the hardest for me to forgive. I've thought a lot about why that is, and I think listening to the Pope this weekend made it clearer to me. It's easier to forgive when someone says they are sorry. Even if that someone isn't the person who hurt you.

Pope Francis also said that he personally took on the evil actions of the clergy who had molested so many, and he personally asked for forgiveness on their behalf. How does that work?

About fifteen years ago, I met with an Orthodox priest and a friend who needed his counsel. She had been hurt by another priest and was struggling to get over it. The priest we were talking with did an amazing thing. He got down on his hands and knees—he prostrated himself before her—and said, "On behalf of any and all clergy who have ever hurt you, please forgive me."

Please forgive me. Powerful words.

But what if they never come? It's so easy to stay mad at someone who never says, "sorry." But who are we hurting by carrying around pain and anger all our lives?

For the past few years I've been keeping a photograph on my bureau, one that used to be stored away in a box. It's a picture of my mother with her father and mother—my grandparents. It was taken around 1932—when my mother was four years old, the same age I was when my grandfather molested me. I have often wondered if he didn't also hurt her—her alcoholic and abusive behavior were telltale signs—but I never asked her. I adored my grandmother, Emma Sue, for whom I was named. And for a while I just wanted the picture because of her. But recently I've found myself stopping in front of it, looking my grandfather in the eyes and saying, "I forgive you." I don't always feel the forgiveness, emotionally, but I believe the words in my heart, and just saying them helps. And now after the Pope's words this weekend, I have a mental image that also helps. When I feel the pain and the anger starting to flare up again, I will think, "God weeps."

Nothing is Really Wrong
2013

On this rainy Monday just before Christmas, I've got a song on my mind that isn't exactly a Christmas carol.

Last week I watched a TV special about Karen and Richard Carpenter. I loved their music back in the late sixties and seventies, and was devastated by Karen's death from anorexia at age 32. As Richard said on the special last week, little was known about eating disorders back then, and by the time Karen went in for treatment, it was too late and she died. I've never known what drove her to anorexia—there were only vague references on the show about the stress she was under with her career. But I found myself weeping as I watched her sing "Rainy Days and Mondays," one of my favorite of their songs. Especially when she sang this verse:

> *What I've got they used to call the blues.*
> *Nothing is really wrong.*
> *Feeling like I don't belong.*
> *Walking around, some kind of lonely clown,*
> *Rainy days and Mondays always get me down.*

My mother used to say she was "blue." I think it was her generation's term for depression. Or maybe for feelings that could grow into depression or just sit there on the soul like a mild sadness. Sadness as an emotion doesn't have to become malignant. But sometimes it overpowers us. And for some of us it's often there. As Karen sings:

What I've got has come and gone before.

No need to talk it out,

We know what it's all about….

Did she? Did she know what it was all about?

I remember a time in my thirties when I wished I had anorexia. Yes. It was becoming prevalent in the news and although I struggled with bulimia and body image distortion and exercise addiction for many years, most of all I wanted to be skinny. And free of my food and body issues. I became severely depressed on and off during that time, and to this day those feelings can overwhelm me at a moment's notice. But as I've gotten older I've learned to deal with my emotions better—and my food cravings.

Anorexia is about control. I've always had control issues, and since control is pretty much an illusion (how many of us really have control over our lives?) those of us who crave it look for ways to tamp down that craving. Or we look for areas in our out-of-control lives where we can create order. Controlling what we eat is one of the ways that we sometimes seek out. Even as I continue the 1000-1200-calorie diet I've been on for three and a half months (and I've lost 15 pounds!) I recognize the high I get when I punch my calories into my LoseIt! app on my iPhone and stay under my limit for the day. And the euphoria when the scales register even another half pound loss is greater than the pleasure of a favorite food or drink. Most of the time.

What a journey I've been on most of my sixty-four years. I'm thankful for my spiritual life, which helps moderate my tendency towards emotional and behavioral imbalance. I still go over my calorie budget occasionally, and some days I give in to that martini that tips the balance a bit too far. But the good days are becoming more frequent than the bad ones, and for that I am thankful.

Even on rainy days and Mondays.

Permissions

The following essays and book excerpts were previously published in various books, journals, magazines, and blogs. They are used here with permission of the author, Susan Cushman. (*Pen & Palette* is the author's personal blog, which can be found at www.susancushman.com.)

"A Soft Opening," *Pen & Palette*, April 30, 2008.

"A Spiritual Home," *Pen & Palette*, October 1, 2015.

"Avery," *Friends of the Library (*Koehler Books, 2009).

"An Unexpected Gift," *Tangles and Plaques: A Mother and Daughter Face Alzheimer's (*eLectio Publishing, 2017).

"Are These My People?" *Muscadine Lines: A Southern Journal*, 2009.

"Blocked," *Santa Fe Writers Project* (literary awards finalist) July 2, 2008.

"Burying Saint Joseph," *skirt!* Magazine, January 2008.

"Chiaroscuro: Shimmer and Shadow," *Circling Faith: Southern Women on Spirituality* (University of Alabama press, 2012).

"Eat, Drink, Repeat: One Woman's Three-Day Search for Everything," *The Shoe Burnin': Stories of Southern Soul*, (Rivers Edge Media, 2013).

"Elizabeth and Lewy Body Dementia," *John and Mary Margaret* (Koehler Books, 2021).

"End-of-Life Issues," *Tangles and Plaques: A Mother and Daughter Face Alzheimer's* (eLectio Publishing, 2017).

"Finding Balance in Orthodoxy," *The Memphis Commercial Appeal*, July 7, 2012

"Flannery O'Connor On Writing and Not Loving God," *Pen & Palette*, December 18, 2015

"God Weeps," *Pen & Palette*, September 28, 2015.

"Hard Labor: The Birth of a Novelist," *Southern Writers on Writing* (University Press of Mississippi, 2018).

"Holy Mother Mary Pray to God For Us," *Pen & Palette*, March 27, 2015.

"Icons Will Save the World," *First Things, the Journal of Religion, Culture and Public Life*, December 20, 2007.

"Living With a Writer's Brokenness," *A Good Blog is Hard to Find*, June 21, 2011.

"Mary of Egypt—the Opera," *Cherry Bomb* (Dogwood Press 2017).

"Mod Barbie, Elphaba, and the Yellow Rose of Texas," *The Pulpwood Queens Celebrate 20 Years!* (Brother Mockingbird Publishing, December 2019).

"Monasteries and Weeping Icons," *Cherry Bomb* (Dogwood Press 2017).

"myPod," *skirt!* Magazine, October 2007.

"Nothing is Really Wrong," *Pen & Palette*, December 21, 2015.

"Six Books in Three Years: An Indie Publishing Journey," *Women Writers, Women's Books*, October 3, 2019.

"Super-Sized Enlightenment," *skirt!* Magazine, November 2008 (republished here as "A Life of Partial Virtue).

"The Crossroads of Circumstance: Setting in Southern Literature," *A Good Blog is Hard to Find*, October 26, 2010.

"The Glasses," *Tangles and Plaques: A Mother and Daughter Face Alzheimer's.* Originally published in *Southern Women's Review*, January 2010.

"The Imperfect Peace," *Southern Stories* (USADeepSouth.com) 2009.

"The New Normal," *Pen & Palette*, July 6 2015.

"The Other Woman," *Mom Writers Literary Magazine*, November 2008.

"The Wind in the Trees," *My Oxford* (Yoknapatawpha Arts Council) 2013.

"Walker, Alzheimer's, and Sunset Park," *John and Mary Margaret* (Koehler Books, 2021).

"Watching," *Saint Katherine Review* (Vol. 1 No. 2) 2011. An abbreviated version of this essay was also published in *Take Care: Tales, Tips, and Love From Women Caregivers* (Braughler Books, 2017).

"Writing *John and Mary Margaret*: Crossing the Color Divide," *Welcome Home Magazine*, March 2022.

"Writing Memoir: Art vs. Confessional," "There Are No Rules," (*Writer's Digest* blog) January 7, 2011.

About the Author

Susan Cushman is a native of Jackson, Mississippi, and has lived in Memphis since 1988. She started her blog, "Pen and Palette," in 2007, and curated sixty of those posts for her first published book, a memoir, *Tangles and Plaques: A Mother and Daughter Face Alzheimer's* (2017). She published seven books in her late sixties, including her recent novel *John and Mary Margaret* (2021).

Susan and her husband of fifty-one years, Bill, who is a physician (aka Dr. William Cushman) and an Orthodox priest (aka Father Basil Cushman), are converts from the Presbyterian Church to the Orthodox Church, which Susan writes about frequently. They have three grown adopted "children," and four mixed-race granddaughters.

Where to follow Susan:

Website: https://susancushman.com/

Facebook: https://www.facebook.com/sjcushman/

Instagram: https://www.instagram.com/sjcushman/

Twitter: https://twitter.com/SusanCushman

Photo by Maude Schuler Clay

CPSIA information can be obtained
at www.ICGtesting.com
Printed in the USA
JSHW052011060422
24600JS00004B/11